BIGGER MUSCLES IN 42 DAYS

Keith Whitley prepares for a high-intensity set of deadlifts.

BIGGER MUSCLES IN 42 DAYS

ELLINGTON DARDEN, PH.D.

PHOTOGRAPHY BY BILL COX

A PERIGEE BOOK

A Perigee Book
Published by The Berkley Publishing Group
A division of Penguin Putnam Inc.
375 Hudson Street
New York, NY 10014

Copyright © 1992 by Ellington Darden, Ph.D.
All rights reserved. This book, or parts thereof,
may not be reproduced in any form without permission.
Published simultaneously in Canada

The Penguin Putnam Inc. World Wide Web site address is
http://www.penguinputnam.com

Library of Congress
Cataloging-in-Publication Data

Darden, Ellington, 1943–.
    Bigger muscles in 42 days / by Ellington Darden:
photographs by Bill Cox.
        p.   cm.
    ISBN 0-399-51706-5 (alk. paper)
    1. Bodybuilding.   I. Title.   II. Title: Bigger muscles in
forty-two days.
    GV546.5.S354   1992   91-14492 CIP
    646.7′5—dc20

Book design © 1992 by Martin Moskof
Cover design © 1992 by Phoebe Lou Sealy
Front and back cover photographs © Bill Cox
Pictured on front and back cover: Keith Whitley

First edition: January 1992

Printed in the United States of America

        13   14   15   16   17   18   19   20

This book is printed on acid-free paper.
        ∞

Other Books of Interest
by Ellington Darden, Ph.D.

BIG
Massive Muscles in 10 Weeks
Super High-Intensity Bodybuilding
The Nautilus Diet
How to Lose Body Fat
Conditioning for Football
The Athlete's Guide to Sports Medicine
The Nautilus Book
The Nautilus Nutrition Book
The Nautilus Woman
The Nautilus Bodybuilding Book
The Nautilus Advanced Bodybuilding Book
The Six-Week Fat-to-Muscle Makeover
Big Arms in Six Weeks
100 High-Intensity Ways to Improve Your Bodybuilding
32 Days to a 32-Inch Waist
Hot Hips and Fabulous Thighs
New High-Intensity Bodybuilding

ACKNOWLEDGMENTS

Special thanks goes to Tom Cunningham who, in addition to
his camera skills, is a longtime gymnast and iron pumper.
While Tom is still an amateur photographer, it was his knowl-
edge of these activities that led to the insights and accu-
racies of many of the pictures in this book. Thanks also to
Noël Pensock of Total Color, Inc., for a beautiful job of printing
the photographs. Appreciation is extended to Roland Jehl and
Hilary Hoffman, owners of the Austin Gym in Richardson,
Texas, where all the training was done.

WARNING!

The high-intensity routines in this book are intended for
healthy men and women. People with health problems should
not follow these routines without a physician's approval.
Before beginning any exercise or nutrition program, always
consult with your doctor.

CONTENTS

Many bodybuilders fail to get maximum results from their training because they do not have a well-designed plan. *Bigger Muscles* contains such a plan, and when followed correctly will produce dramatic results.

GETTING BIGGER!

- **INCREDIBLE MUSCULAR SIZE.**
- **AWESOME ARMS AND CHEST.**
- **MASSIVE THIGHS.**
- **BIGGER, STRONGER BODY PARTS.**

These are the bodybuilder's goals.

Few bodybuilders, however, reach their goals. Most fall short because they stray from the basics. In their quest for massive muscles, they blitz and bomb, rotate the split, and amino acid their bodies into a deep state of overtraining. They train too much, load their bodies with excessive protein, and rest too little.

The vast majority of bodybuilders fail to get the results that they desperately desire. In short, they do not get bigger!

This book contains a program that can remedy that situation.

BIGGER MUSCLES is a continuation of my last book— *BIG.* In *BIG,* I trained Eddie Mueller, a 23-year-old athlete from Florida. In six weeks, Eddie's body weight increased from 172½ to 192, for a gain of 19½ pounds. While Eddie was certainly satisfied with his gains, he still wanted more size.

BIGGER is designed to help Eddie move closer to reaching his full potential. Not only is *BIGGER* for intermediate bodybuilders like Eddie Mueller, but it's also for beginners and advanced trainees.

In this program I wanted to test some new twists on training, which I thought would stimulate even faster growth than was produced in *BIG.* One of the new twists is called contra-lateral. Contra-lateral training involves working the right side of your upper body and the left side of your lower body on one day, and the left side of your upper body and right lower body on the next day. More will be said about this new breakthrough later, but let me simply say that the results are amazing.

I believe you'll find the complete course in this book equally amazing. Everything is included for building massive muscles fast!

To prove the effectiveness of this new course, I personally trained two bodybuilders from the Austin Gym in Dallas, Texas. The first was Keith Whitley, an experienced bodybuilder who had placed second in the 1986 AAU Mr. America contest and fifth in the 1986 Mr. World contest. The second was David Hammond, an 18-year-old novice who had been training for a year. Both had good bodybuilding potential and both were willing to work hard to obtain the best-possible results.

From my past experiences in working with thousands of bodybuilders, I knew that being specific with both exercising and eating are keys to success. This program, however, would go many steps further. Not only would Keith and David be directed in their exercising and eating, but also in their resting, relaxing, and even thinking to a certain extent.

They would be tested and measured—before and after—on such parameters as body fat, lean muscle mass, resting metabolic rate, body part size, and strength. Diaries and records would be kept. All the important aspects would be photographed. Each phase of the getting-bigger process, no matter how small, would be accounted for.

As I look back on my bodybuilding career, which spans over 30 years, early on I wished I would have had a more specific plan to follow. A plan that showed me exactly what to do: exercises, routines, equipment, food, supplements, rest, relaxation, and reading matter on a daily basis.

I wish I would have had a book like *BIGGER MUS-CLES.* Because *BIGGER MUSCLES* provides a day-to-day plan of exactly what to do for 42 days to get as big and as strong as possible.

The main part of the book consists of 42 chapters. There's a chapter to utilize each day for six weeks. You'll be able to follow the specific schedule that Keith Whitley and David Hammond employed to pack on over 25 pounds of mass to each of their bodies . . . in only 42 days!

Before the actual 42-day plan is presented, let's briefly cover the latest facts about bodybuilding exercise and nutrition.

With the exercise and nutrition program described in this book, Keith Whitley went from a body weight of 246 to 280.3, an increase of 34.3 pounds.

High-Intensity exercise carries each set to the point of momentary muscular failure.

BIGGER BASICS: EXERCISE

It's happening in California. It's happening in New York, Florida, and Texas.

In just about every bodybuilding gym you visit throughout the United States—or the world for that matter—trainees perform their exercises in a sloppy, inefficient manner. They cheat on the lifting and neglect the lowering. In the process they arch their backs, move their elbows, dip their shoulders, bounce the bar off their chests, and do dozens of little things that make the exercises easier.

In actuality, they should be doing little things to make the exercises harder. Harder exercises, not easier, is what stimulates muscular growth.

In gyms across the country bodybuilders spend hours a day training in styles which do little to permit growth. In fact, many of their techniques actually produce losses in size and strength.

What is needed is a return to the basics, the basics of what stimulates a muscle to grow and how to follow through with the growth.

WHAT MAKES A MUSCLE GROW

The scientific term for muscular growth is *hypertrophy*. Its inverse, called *atrophy*, refers to the breakdown of muscle tissue from neglect or lack of use. Atrophy involves the metabolic breakdown of muscle into its constituent compounds, which are then eliminated by the bloodstream.

Hypertrophy, or muscular growth, occurs as a result of increased demands placed on the muscle. The signal for growth is clearly intense overload. When a muscle is forced with high-intensity requirements, it responds with a protective increase in size and strength.

A number of changes associated with hypertrophy explain increased muscular size and strength:

- The actin and particularly the myosin protein filaments enlarge.
- The number of myofibrils increases.
- The number of blood capillaries within the fiber may become more numerous.
- The amount of connective tissue within the muscle may thicken.

Some or all of these changes within a muscle must take place at the cellular level. Three factors govern cellular stimulation. First, the targeted muscle must be stimulated to grow through proper exercise. Second, the muscle must be permitted to grow with adequate rest. Third, the muscle must be supplied with the necessary nutrients to grow.

Exercise, *rest*, and *nutrients*—in that order—are the key requirements for muscular growth. The difficult part is getting the just right balance, without having too little or too much of any factor.

INTENSITY: OFTEN THE IGNORED FACTOR

"If you've never vomited from a set of barbell curls," says Arthur Jones, the inventor of Nautilus equipment, "then you don't know the meaning of intense exercise."

Keith Whitley summed it up best in a comment he made to Betsy Hoffmann, a champion in women's bodybuilding.

"Is that high-intensity training really working?"

Betsy asked Keith. Keith was halfway through the 42-day program and had already packed on over 20 pounds.

"I'll say it's working," replied Keith. "It's the hardest training I've ever done. Most people in the gym can't push themselves to the level that Dr. Darden pushes me. But that's the secret: getting those last one or two repetitions, and Doc makes sure I do them."

Keith is correct. Those last repetitions are the most important.

The first several repetitions in a set are simply preparation, a warm-up, for those last repetitions. For maximum growth stimulation, you must always attempt the momentarily impossible.

If you can do another repetition, do it. And if you complete it, try one more. Do not stop until additional upward movement is impossible. When no upward movement is possible, keep pushing and breathing for another 15 seconds. Maybe, just maybe, the weight will move upward a fraction of an inch.

Evidently, growth stimulation is similar to turning on an electric light. A flick of the switch turns on the light immediately, not gradually. But it takes working through those last, painful repetitions to finally get to the switch. And even then you may fail to flick if you don't attempt—for 15 seconds—the momentarily impossible.

Once the switch is turned on and growth is activated, then more sets are not necessary. More sets can even be detrimental because they use up your valuable recovery ability.

So don't avoid the last repetitions in your exercise. Look forward to the increased intensity, endure the pain, and reap the results.

It's impossible to build quality muscle without hard work. Too many bodybuilders are not willing to work hard enough to get maximum muscle size. Don't be one of them.

Decide now that exercising intensely is the best way to get bigger.

PROGRESSION: KEEP IT SIMPLE

Continual muscular growth depends on progress being made at each workout. Progress is best measured by a workout-by-workout increase in the weight used, or the number of repetitions performed, on each exercise.

The rule to remember is as follows: Perform between 4 and 8 repetitions of each exercise. Any time you can do 8 or more repetitions in proper form, increase the resistance by 5 percent at the next workout.

Always try to do at least one more repetition per exercise today than you did in the same exercise during the previous workout. And always use as much weight as possible, as much weight as possible in good form.

GOOD FORM: SLOWER IS BETTER

In my travels throughout the world, I seldom see good form being practiced. Slamming, banging, and bouncing the weights, as opposed to smooth, slow lifting and lowering, seems to be the choice of most trainees. Once bad form is established, it's difficult to change. But change you must, especially if you want maximum growth stimulation.

Good form requires a very slow speed of lifting and a smooth lowering. No sudden, quick, or explosive movements are permitted. The idea is to keep your targeted muscles overloaded throughout the entire set.

Effective overload best occurs when the positive or lifting phase of each repetition is performed in 10 seconds. The negative or lowering phase is done in 5 seconds.

- 10 seconds up
- 5 seconds down

In other words, each repetition should take at least 15 seconds.

Such a style of training is called *super slow*.

Super-slow training is the most efficient way to stimulate your muscles to grow larger and stronger. It's the best way to get bigger.

Why is super-slow training better than faster styles of lifting? Because it eliminates most of the momentum from each repetition. Eliminating the momentum better isolates the involved muscles and makes the exercise harder.

Remember, the harder and the more targeted the exercise is, the better.

DURATION: HARDER AND BRIEFER

Once the intensity of your exercise is high and your form is slow and smooth, then the length of your workouts must be brief. Rarely do I have any of my trainees perform more than 16 total exercises in any workout. One set, and one set only, is usually the rule. Once again, that one set is carried to absolute momentary muscular failure, until no upward movement is possible.

If your workouts, from start to finish, are taking longer than one hour to complete, then you are not training hard enough or you are taking too much time between exercises. None of the workouts in this book take longer than one hour to finish. In fact, once you get the hang of each one, you should be able to complete it in 45 minutes or less.

The idea is to get in and out of the gym effectively and efficiently. Doing so supplies your body with maximum growth stimulation and maximum recovery ability.

SUMMARIZING THE BASICS

The basic information that you will need for getting bigger from exercise can be summarized as follows:

- Continue doing each exercise until no upward movement is possible. A final effort of holding the weight stationary for another 15 seconds increases the intensity.
- Work between 4 and 8 repetitions. When 8 or more repetitions are done in good form, add 5 percent more resistance at the next workout.
- Perform each repetition in the super-slow style. Lift the weight slowly in 10 seconds. Lower the weight smoothly in 5 seconds.
- Keep your workouts brief. One set of 16 or fewer exercises applies in most situations.

A slow speed of movement leads to more muscle fiber involvement and thus more growth stimulation.

Super-slow squats are so demanding that they must be performed infrequently.

The relative size of 5 pounds of fat (left) and 5 pounds of muscle is shown in this picture. Muscle is approximately 20 percent denser than fat, and therefore takes up less space.

Carbohydrate-rich foods—such as fruits, vegetables, breads, and cereals—should be over 50 percent of a body-builder's diet.

BIGGER BASICS: NUTRITION

Both exercise and nutrition should be balanced as a team to optimize the muscular growth process. Bodybuilders must be prepared to meet the special demands they make on their bodies. This requires nutritious food and sound eating habits.

The basics of nutritious food and sound eating habits begin with a description of the essential nutrients.

NUTRIENTS

Some fifty different nutrients are found in foods, but they can be grouped under six main headings: proteins, minerals, vitamins, fats, carbohydrates, and water.

Proteins, fats, and carbohydrates are the energy-supplying nutrients. Energy from food is typically measured as heat and expressed as calories. Fat contains over twice as many calories as an equal amount of protein and carbohydrate.

1 gram of fat	=	9 calories
1 gram of protein	=	4 calories
1 gram of carbohydrate	=	4 calories

Although most foods contain more than one nutrient, no single food contains all the nutrients in the amounts the body needs. That is why you need to eat a variety of foods each day.

PROTEINS

All humans require protein to sustain life. It is the chief tissue builder and the basic substance of every cell in your body. You need protein all through life for the maintenance and repair of body tissues.

Protein is made up of smaller units called amino acids. When foods are digested, the proteins are broken down into amino acids, which are then re-arranged to form the many special and distinct proteins in your body.

The proteins in food are usually made up of eighteen or more different kinds of amino acids. Your body can make its own supply of more than half of these. The others, called essential amino acids, must come ready-made from the foods you eat. The amino acid composition of protein determines its nutritional value. Highest in value are proteins that supply all the essential amino acids in approximately the proportions needed by your body. Generally, these proteins are in foods of animal origin: meat, fish, poultry, eggs, and milk.

Proteins from grains, vegetables, and fruits supply valuable amounts of many amino acids but fewer than do animal proteins. Proteins from legumes, especially soybeans and chickpeas, are almost as good as proteins from animal sources.

For a bodybuilder's daily meals, only a portion of the protein needs to come from animal sources. Combining cereal and vegetable foods with a little meat or other sources of animal protein will improve the protein value of the meal. Examples of nourishing combinations are cereal with milk, rice with fish, spaghetti with meat sauce, and vegetable stew with meat. Or you could simply have milk as a beverage along with foods of plant origin. It is good to have some food from animal sources at each meal.

MINERALS

Many minerals are required by your body. They give strength and rigidity to certain tissues and help with numerous vital functions.

■ Calcium

Calcium is the most abundant mineral element in your body. Teamed with phosphorus, it is largely responsible for the hardness of bones and teeth. About 99 percent of the calcium in the body is found in these two tissues.

The small amount of calcium in your body tissues and fluids aids in the proper functioning of your heart, muscles, and nerves, and helps your blood coagulate if you are bleeding.

Milk is an outstanding source of calcium. Appreciable amounts are contributed by cheese, especially Cheddar types. Calcium is found in ice cream, collards, kale, mustard greens, turnip greens, and canned salmon.

■ Iodine

People who live far away from the seacoast in areas where the soil is low in iodine sometimes fail to get an adequate supply of this mineral. An iodine deficiency can cause goiter, a swelling of the thyroid gland.

Iodized salt and seafoods are reliable sources of iodine. Regular use of iodized salt is the most practical way to put enough iodine in your diet.

■ Iron

Iron is needed by your body in relatively small but vital amounts. It combines with protein to make hemoglobin, which carries oxygen from the lungs to body cells and removes carbon dioxide from the cells. Iron also helps the cells obtain energy from food.

Only a few foods contain much iron. Liver is a particularly good source. Lean meats, heart, kidney, shellfish, dry beans, dry peas, dark green vegetables, dried fruit, egg yolks, and molasses are also reliable sources.

■ Other Essential Minerals

Two other minerals with vitally important functions are phosphorus and magnesium. Like calcium, they are found in largest amounts in bones and teeth. Among their other functions, they play an indispensable role in your body's use of food for energy.

Magnesium is found in adequate amounts in nuts, whole-grain products, dry beans, dry peas, and dark green vegetables. Phosphorus is found in a variety of foods. If your meals contain foods that provide enough protein and calcium, you very likely will get enough phosphorus as well.

Ten or more additional minerals are essential in keeping your body functioning smoothly. These minerals, however, are usually obtained in satisfactory amounts by a well-chosen variety of foods.

VITAMINS

Vitamins play a dynamic role in bodily processes. They take part in the release of energy from foods, promote normal growth of different kinds of tissue, and are essential to the proper functioning of nerves and muscles.

Thirteen separate, necessary vitamins have been identified. Should you consume vitamin pills to be sure you get enough of each one? As a rule the answer is *no*. A healthy athlete can get all the necessary vitamins from a properly selected and prepared diet.

Although concentrated vitamins are available at stores as pills or capsules, these should not be taken unless your doctor recommends them. If you take vitamins without your doctor's advice, you may be spending money needlessly. Your body can make use of only so much of each vitamin. Excesses either are excreted as wastes or may accumulate and be detrimental to your health.

Taking vitamins without medical advice may encourage you to rely on these vitamins to make your daily diet complete and thus to neglect those foods that contain not only vitamins but other valuable nutrients as well.

Here is a summary of the vitamins, including some of their functions and a list of foods that are dependable sources.

■ Vitamin A

Vitamin A is present only in foods of animal origin. Many vegetables and fruits, however, particularly green and yellow ones, contain a substance called carotene that your body can change into vitamin A.

Liver is an outstanding source of vitamin A. Important amounts are also found in eggs, butter, margarine, whole milk, and cheese made with whole milk. Carotene is found in largest amounts in dark green vegetables and deep yellow vegetables and fruits.

■ B Vitamins

Three of the B vitamins, thiamin, riboflavin, and niacin, play a central role in the release of energy from food. They also help with proper functioning of nerves, normal appetite, good digestion, and healthy skin.

Foods in the meat group are leading sources of these vitamins. Whole-grain and enriched bread and cereals supply smaller but important amounts. A few foods are outstanding sources: milk for riboflavin, lean pork for thiamin, and organ meats for all three.

Getting enough niacin is not a problem if enough protein is included in daily meals. An essential amino acid, tryptophan, is present in protein and can be changed by the body into niacin.

Other B vitamins, B6 and particularly B12 and folic acid, help prevent anemia. Vitamin B12 is found only in foods of animal origin. Folic acid is present in largest amounts in organ meats and dark green leafy vegetables. Good sources of vitamin B6 include meats, whole-grain cereals, dry beans, potatoes, and dark green leafy vegetables.

■ Vitamin C (Ascorbic Acid)

Ascorbic acid helps form and maintain cementing material that holds your body cells together and strengthens the walls of blood vessels. It also assists in normal tooth and bone formation and aids in healing wounds.

Oranges, grapefruit, lemons, and fresh strawberries are rich in ascorbic acid. Other important sources include tomatoes, broccoli, cabbage, cantaloupe, cauliflower, green and red peppers, some dark green leafy vegetables, and watermelon.

■ Vitamin D

Vitamin D is important in building strong bones and teeth because it enables your body to use the calcium and phosphorus supplied by food.

Few foods contain much vitamin D naturally. Milk with vitamin D added is a practical source. Small amounts of vitamin D are present in egg yolks, butter, and liver. Larger amounts are present in sardines, salmon, herring, and tuna.

Another source is the vitamin D produced by the chemical reaction of direct sunlight on your skin.

■ Other Vitamins

Combinations of food that sufficiently provide for the vitamins above are likely to furnish enough of the other vitamins not specified.

FATS

Weight for weight, fats provide more than twice as much energy, or calories, as either carbohydrates or proteins. They also carry the fat-soluble vitamins A, D, E, and K, and they perform the following functions:

■ Make up part of the structure of cells.
■ Form a protective cushion around vital organs.
■ Spare protein for bodybuilding and repair by providing energy.
■ Supply an essential fatty-linoleic acid.

Your body does not manufacture linoleic acid; it must be provided by food. It is found in substantial amounts in many oils that come from plants—particularly corn, cottonseed, safflower, sesame, soybean, and wheat germ. These are referred to as polyunsaturated fats. Margarines, salad dressings, mayonnaise, and cooking oils are usually made from one or more of these oils. Nuts contain less linoleic acid than do most vegetable oils. Among the nuts, walnuts rate quite high. Poultry and fish oils have more linoleic acid than other animal fats, which rank fairly low as sources. In choosing daily meals, it is best to keep the total amount of fat at a moderate level and to include some foods that contain polyunsaturated fats.

In cooking, fats add flavor and variety to many foods. Fats also make foods and meals satisfying because they digest slowly and delay the feeling of hunger.

Common sources of fats are butter, margarine, shortening, cooking and salad oils, cream, most cheeses, mayonnaise, salad dressing, nuts, bacon, and other fatty meats. Meats, whole milk, eggs, and chocolate contain some fat naturally. Many popular snacks, baked goods, pastries, and other desserts are made with fat or are cooked with it.

CARBOHYDRATES

Foods supply carbohydrates chiefly in three forms: starches, sugars, and cellulose, or fibrous, materials. Starches and sugars are major sources of energy for humans. Cellulose furnish bulk in the diet.

Glucose, commonly called blood sugar, is the main form in which starches and sugars are used by cells to furnish energy for bodily processes and to support activity and growth. This spares the proteins for tissue building and repair and for other special jobs. Carbohydrates also help your body to digest fats efficiently.

The chief sources of starch are grains such as wheat, oats, corn, and rice. Starches made from grains are flour, macaroni, spaghetti, noodles, grits, breads, and breakfast cereals. Potatoes, sweet potatoes, and dry beans and peas are also good sources of starch.

Most other vegetables, fruits, and fruit juices contain smaller amounts of carbohydrates. In vegetables, the carbohydrate is mainly in the form of starches; in fruits, it is chiefly sugars. Cane and beet sugars, jellies, jam, candy and other sweets, honey, molasses, and syrups are concentrated sources of sugar.

WATER

Water is essential for life. It ranks next to air, or oxygen, in importance. Your body's need for water even exceeds your need for food. You can live for days, even weeks, without food, but only a few days without water.

About one-half to two-thirds of your body is made up of water. Water is the medium of body fluids, secretions, and excretions. It carries food materials from one part of your body to the other.

Water is also the solvent for all products of digestion, which move through your intestinal wall in a water solution, passing into the bloodstream for use throughout your body. Water also carries wastes from your body. Your body temperature is regulated by the evaporation of water through your skin and lungs.

It takes a regular and generous intake of water to perform all these jobs. Your body gets water from many sources. The most obvious is the water you drink, but this often represents only a small part of the total intake. Water also comes in coffee, tea, juice, soft drinks, milk, and soups. Foods, such as vegetables, fruits, meat, and even bread and dry cereal, contain some water. And water is formed when your body uses food for energy.

DAILY FOOD GUIDE FOR BALANCED NUTRITION

Bodybuilders need adequate amounts of proteins, minerals, vitamins, fats, carbohydrates, and water on a daily basis. Balanced nutrition generally means that you are consuming the appropriate servings each day from the basic four food groups.

The eating plan that I've used successfully many times previously with bodybuilders is called the 4:4:8:8 ratio. The 4:4:8:8 ratio is a reminder of how much of each food group you should have as a minimum each day.

- 4 servings from the meat/poultry/fish/legumes/egg group—referred to in abbreviation form as the Meat Group.
- 4 servings from the milk/yogurt/cheese group—referred to as the Milk Group.
- 8 servings from the Fruit/Vegetable Group.
- 8 servings from the Bread/Cereal Group (which includes rice and pasta).

The carbohydrate-rich foods—fruits, vegetables, breads, and cereals—provide significant vitamins and minerals. The protein-rich foods—meat and milk—supply adequate amino acids for muscular growth. The 4:4:8:8 ratio is perfect for getting bigger.

Thus, most of the menus and meal schedules in this program are derived by using the 4:4:8:8 ratio. It worked well for Keith Whitley and David Hammond. And it will work for you!

In the next chapter, I'll describe how I determine the number of calories for Keith and David to consume each day, and how you can do the same. Plus, I'll discuss the day-by-day workout program.

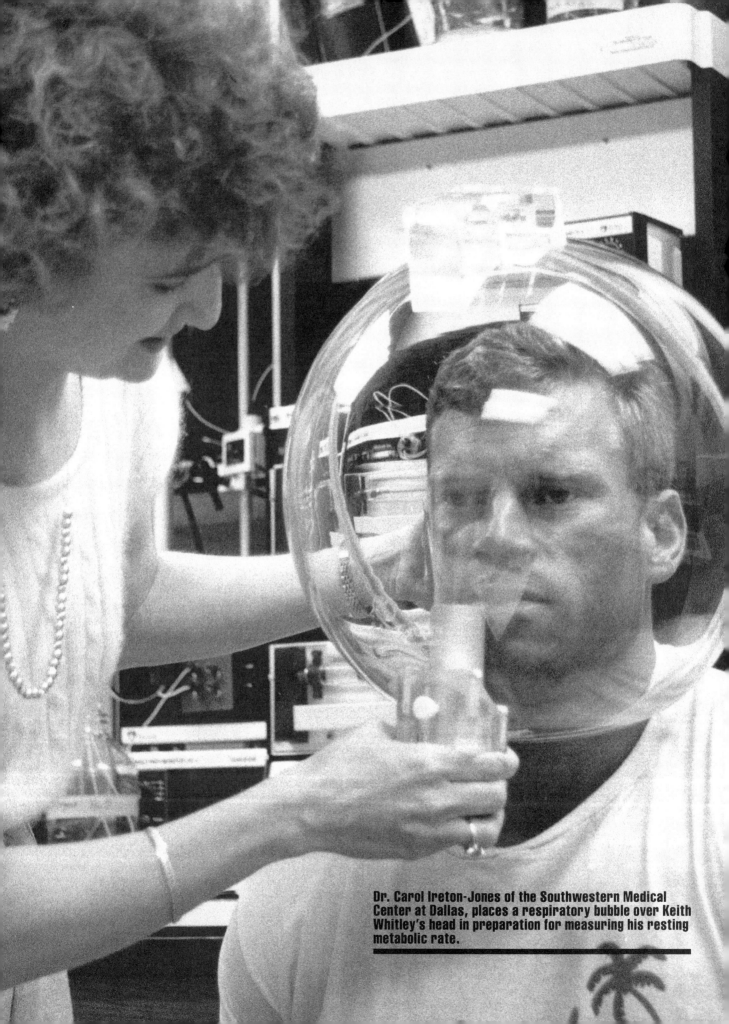

Dr. Carol Ireton-Jones of the Southwestern Medical Center at Dallas, places a respiratory bubble over Keith Whitley's head in preparation for measuring his resting metabolic rate.

THE BIGGER PROGRAM: WEEK BY WEEK

THE EATING PLAN

Resting metabolic rate is the total energy output of the body under resting conditions and after a six-hour fast. Resting metabolism is important because knowing Keith's and David's would allow me to determine the optimum number of calories that each could consume daily without putting on significant fatty tissue.

To accurately calculate resting metabolic rate I needed laboratory equipment to measure the amount of oxygen consumed and carbon dioxide expelled. The University of Texas Southwestern Medical Center at Dallas has such equipment and I called on Dr. Carol Ireton-Jones, a research dietitian, to supervise the testing. Both Keith and David were assessed on October 2, 1990.

Keith, at a height of 6'1" and a weight of 246 pounds, had a resting metabolic rate of 3,029 calories per day. David, at a height of 5'10½" and a weight of 186 pounds, registered a rate of 1,859 calories per day. Remember, 3,029 and 1,859 were the number of cal-

ories per day that Keith and David were spending at a *resting* state. I therefore needed to go several steps further and calculate their total energy expenditure by accounting for their activity level, exercise endeavors, and food processing.

Both Keith and David had sedentary jobs, so I took 50 percent of their resting metabolic rates (1,513 and 930 calories, respectively) as their activity levels. I figured Keith burned approximately 500 calories per workout and 500 more to digest his food per day. I estimated David's workouts at 300 calories each and his food processing at another 300 calories.

Thus, far Keith's total was 5,539 calories and David's was 3,389. Since Keith was 31 years old and David was only 18, I knew Keith was more efficient than David, so I made a slight adjustment for that.

In the final analysis, I established their total daily expenditure, with a little extra for growth, as follows:

Keith Whitley—	David Hammond—
5,500 cal/day for Week 1	3,700 cal/day for Week 1
6,000 cal/day for Week 2	4,000 cal/day for Week 2
6,500 cal/day for Week 3	4,300 cal/day for Week 3
7,000 cal/day for Week 4	4,600 cal/day for Week 4
7,500 cal/day for Week 5	4,900 cal/day for Week 5
8,000 cal/day for Week 6	5,200 cal/day for Week 6

Notice that with each succeeding week I added an extra 500 calories per day to Keith's and an extra 300 calories per day to David's total. This progression allowed for the additon of several pounds of muscle per week. (See charts on pages 24–27.)

At the end of the second and fourth weeks I planned to take additional skinfold calculations to determine whether the calories per day that Keith and David were consuming were too little, just right, or too many. I expected each to deposit from one-half to one pound of fat per week, as it appears that doing so actually assists the muscle-building process.

FIGURING YOUR CALORIE EXPENDITURE

How can you determine your total caloric expenditure per day and per week, especially since you probably don't have access to the metabolic measuring equipment? Here is the method I recommend:

■ Take your body weight in pounds,
■ Multiply this number by 20.

This provides you with a good estimate of the total number of calories you burn per day. Consuming this approximate number each day should keep your body weight relatively stable.

To add muscular mass, you not only have to exercise intensely, but you must also eat slightly more calories to supply the needed growth nutrients.

Thus, to your total above I recommend that you add extra calories each succeeding week as did Keith and David. Here are my suggestions:

If you weigh:

■ 200 pounds or under, add 300 each week
■ 201–225 pounds, add 400 each week
■ 226 pounds or over, add 500 each week

For example, if you weigh 165 pounds, then your estimated calorie expenditure per day should be

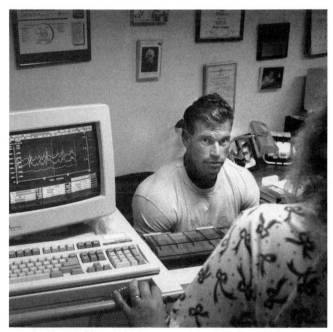

Some of the data used to determine Keith's resting energy expenditure is shown on the monitor.

20×165, or 3,300 calories. Your six-week BIGGER plan would be as follows:

3,600 cal/day for Week 1
3,900 cal/day for Week 2
4,200 cal/day for Week 3
4,500 cal/day for Week 4
4,800 cal/day for Week 5
5,100 cal/day for Week 6

To facilitate the eating process and the record keeping and servings involved, I organized daily diet sheets as guidelines for Keith and David to follow. This assured the proper balance among carbohydrates, fats, and proteins according to the 4:4:4:8 ratio of food groups. Examples from Week 1 and Week 6 are presented on pages 24–27.

Notice that since the Keith was consuming daily well over 5,000 calories, a high-calorie shake of from 1,800 to 2,800 calories per day was frequently used to supplement his normal food intake. Several recipes for such a shake are included on Day 26.

THE EXERCISE PLAN

Both Keith and David, in much of their previous training, had been using a split routine. I'm not a big believer in splitting your workout into lower body one day and upper body the next day, or into any of the various ways of separating the body into workouts. It makes sense to me that your body works best, and grows best, if you exercise it as a whole and rest it in its entirety.

My goal with Keith and David was to start with a split routine and gradually move them to training their entire body on a three-day-per-week schedule. Here is the plan that I organized:

Weeks 1 and 2—Three-days-in-a-row split routine, six days per week.

Monday and Thursday:
  Legs, lower back, abdominals
Tuesday and Friday:
  Shoulders, upper back, chest
Wednesday and Saturday:
  Upper arms, forearms, neck

Weeks 3 and 4—Contra-lateral split routine, five days per week, then four days per week.

Week 3, Monday and Wednesday: right lower body, left upper body
Week 3, Tuesday and Thursday: left lower body, right upper body
Week 3, Saturday: right lower body, left upper body; left lower body, right upper body
Week 4, Monday and Thursday: right lower body, left upper body
Week 4, Tuesday and Friday: left lower body, right upper body

Weeks 5 and 6—Three days a week whole body routine with emphasis on the negative.

Monday, Wednesday, Friday: Legs, shoulders, upper back, chest, biceps, triceps.

I personally trained both Keith and David through all of their weekly workouts. A record of Keith's daily schedule and his workout-by-workout exercises, poundages, repetitions, and progress are listed in the 42-day section. Some of his favorite recipes also are included.

A listing with appropriate blank spaces is presented after Keith's so you can keep records of your day-to-day progress. It's your responsibility to plan, organize, and keep track of your eating, exercising, and resting for the next 42 days.

Doing so will assure the best-possible results. It will guarantee that you will get bigger.

BASIC FOUR FOOD GROUPS FOR BODYBUILDERS

BASIC FOOD Group	MINIMUM DAILY Servings	Serving Size	Food Sources
Meat	4	2–3 ozs. cooked	Meat, poultry, fish
		2 medium	Eggs
		2 tablespoons	Peanut butter
		½ cup	Cottage cheese
		1 cup	Dried beans or peas
Milk	4	1 cup	Milk, yogurt
		1½ ozs.	Cheese
		1–1¾ cups	Milk-containing foods
Fruit/ Vegetable	8	½ cup raw or cooked	Fruit or vegetable
		½ cup juice	Fruit or vegetable
		1 cup raw	Dark green leafy or yellow vegetable
Bread/ Cereal	8	1 slice	Breads: whole-grain and enriched, muffins, rolls
		½–¾ cup	Cereals: cooked, dry, whole-grain, grits, barley, flours
		½ cup	Pasta: macaroni, noodles, spaghetti
		½ cup	Rice: brown or white
Other Foods	6*	1 teaspoon	Butter, margarine, oil
		1 teaspoon	Salad dressing
		2 teaspoons	Jellies, jams, and other sweet toppings Alcohol (not recommended)

May be adjusted up or down depending on daily caloric needs.

On Monday and Wednesday of Week 3, you'll train the left side of your lower body and the right side of your upper body. You'll work the contra-lateral sides on Tuesday and Thursday.

DR. ELLINGTON DARDEN'S BIGGER DIET: for Keith

WEEK 1 FOOD GROUPS	TOTAL CALORIES: 5,500 PER DAY (Add 1,800 Calorie Shake)	DATE: RECOMMENDED DAILY SERVINGS

MEAT

☐ ☐ ☐ ☐ ☐ ☐
☐

6.5

MILK

☐ ☐ ☐ ☐ ☐ ☐

6

FRUIT/ VEGETABLE

☐ ☐ ☐ ☐ ☐ ☐
☐ ☐ ☐ ☐ ☐ ☐
☐

12.5

BREAD/ CEREAL

☐ ☐ ☐ ☐ ☐ ☐
☐ ☐ ☐ ☐ ☐ ☐
☐

12.5

OTHER FOODS

☐ ☐ ☐ ☐ ☐ ☐
☐

7

DR. ELLINGTON DARDEN'S BIGGER DIET: for Keith

| WEEK 6
FOOD GROUPS | TOTAL CALORIES: 8,000 PER DAY
(Add 2,800 Calorie Shake) | DATE:
RECOMMENDED DAILY SERVINGS |

FOOD GROUP							RECOMMENDED DAILY SERVINGS
MEAT	☐	☐	☐	☐	☐	☐	
	☐	☐	☐				8.5
MILK	☐	☐	☐	☐	☐	☐	
	☐	☐					8
FRUIT/ VEGETABLE	☐	☐	☐	☐	☐	☐	
	☐	☐	☐	☐	☐	☐	
	☐	☐	☐	☐	☐	☐	18
BREAD/ CEREAL	☐	☐	☐	☐	☐	☐	
	☐	☐	☐	☐	☐	☐	
	☐	☐	☐	☐	☐	☐	18
OTHER FOODS	☐	☐	☐	☐	☐	☐	
	☐	☐	☐	☐	☐	☐	12

DR. ELLINGTON DARDEN'S BIGGER DIET: for David

MEAT

6.5

MILK

6

FRUIT/ VEGETABLE

12.5

BREAD/ CEREAL

12.5

OTHER FOODS

7

DR. ELLINGTON DARDEN'S BIGGER DIET: for David

WEEK 6   **TOTAL CALORIES: 5,200 PER DAY**   **DATE:**
FOOD GROUPS   RECOMMENDED DAILY SERVINGS

MEAT

8.5

MILK

8

**FRUIT/
VEGETABLE**

18

**BREAD/
CEREAL**

18

**OTHER
FOODS**

12

DR. ELLINGTON DARDEN'S *BIGGER* PROGRAM

NAME		AGE	
	BEFORE	AFTER	DIFFERENCE
Date	_____	_____	
Height	_____	_____	
Weight	_____	_____	_____

CIRCUMFERENCE MEASUREMENTS

Neck	_____	_____	_____
Right upper arm	_____	_____	_____
Left upper arm	_____	_____	_____
Right forearm	_____	_____	_____
Left forearm	_____	_____	_____
Chest	_____	_____	_____
Waist	_____	_____	_____
Hips	_____	_____	_____
Right thigh	_____	_____	_____
Left thigh	_____	_____	_____
Right calf	_____	_____	_____
Left calf	_____	_____	_____

SKINFOLD MEASUREMENTS

Right chest	_____	_____	_____
Right abdomen	_____	_____	_____
Right thigh	_____	_____	_____

TOTAL	_____	_____	_____
PERCENTAGE	_____	_____	_____

BEFORE GETTING STARTED: TAKING MEASUREMENTS

Bodybuilders frequently use measurements as a source of inspiration.

Who in bodybuilding wouldn't like to have 20-inch arms, a 58-inch chest, and 30-inch thighs?

The truth is that most measurements are taken incorrectly, grossly exaggerated, or lied about. Accurately measured, an 18-inch arm is big. A 19-inch arm is very big. And anything above 19 inches must be seen to be believed.

In my bodybuilding research, which spans over 30 years, I've seen only four muscular arms that actually measured 20 inches or larger. Those four arms belonged to Sergio Oliva, Ray Mentzer, Ed Robinson, and Keith Whitley. And each of these men weighed in excess of 230 pounds when their arms were taped.

Measurements are useful in evaluating the present state of your physique. To be of value they must be accurate and repeatable. That's why it's important to understand and apply the following guidelines in measuring your body. Be sure and do them before your first workout and record them on page 28.

You'll need a plastic tape that is 60 inches in length. It's easier to take the measurements if you team up with a friend. Have him do yours, and you take his.

When taking the measurements, apply the tape lightly to the skin. The tape should be taut but not tight. Take duplicate measurements to the nearest one-eighth of an inch at each of the sites and use the average figure as your circumference score.

Do not pump your muscle prior to taking your measurements. Do not take them after a workout. Record all your circumference readings before you exercise.

CIRCUMFERENCES
- **NECK:** Pass the tape around the neck at a level just above the Adam's apple. Make sure the tape is horizontal and neck is relaxed.
- **UPPER ARMS:** Stand and contract the right biceps. The upper arm should be parallel to the floor. Pass the tape around the largest part of the biceps with the tape perpendicular to the upper arm bone. Measure the left biceps in the same manner.
- **FOREARMS:** Extend your elbow completely, make a fist, bend your wrist, and contract the right forearm muscles. Place the tape around largest part of the forearm, perpendicular to the bones in the lower arm. Measure the left forearm in the same manner.
- **CHEST:** Stand erect. Pass the tape around the back at nipple level and bring it together in the front. Keep the tape in a horizontal plane.

- **WAIST:** Pass the tape around the waist at navel level. Keep the tape in a horizontal plane. Do not pull in the belly.
- **HIPS:** Stand erect and look straight ahead, heels together, with weight distributed equally in both feet. Place the tape around the hips at the position of maximum protrusion of the buttocks. Keep the tape in a horizontal plane.
- **THIGHS:** Stand erect, heels approximately shoulder-width apart, with weight distributed equally on both feet. Pass the tape around the right thigh just below the buttocks. Keep the tape in a horizontal plane. Do not contract the thigh muscles. Measure the left thigh in the same manner.
- **CALVES:** Stand erect, heels approximately shoulder-width apart, with weight distributed equally on both feet. Pass the tape around the right calf at the widest point. Keep the tape in a horizontal plane. Do not contract the calf muscles. Measure the left calf in the same manner.

SKINFOLDS
The easiest way to estimate the amount of fat you have on your body is by using a skinfold caliper. You should be able to get this test done at your local YMCA or fitness center. I use the Lange caliper and take the sum of three skinfolds: chest, abdomen, and thigh for men; or triceps, hip, and thigh for women. See the *Research Quarterly for Exercise and Sport* (52: 380–384, 1981) to determine your percentage of body fat by the use of a simple nomogram.

The idea is to make sure your body fat does not increase significantly during the 42-day program. Monitoring your body fat level every 10–14 days will let you know if it is stable or on the rise.

A lean, well-defined bodybuilder will have a body-fat level of under 10 percent. Some champions even get below 5 percent.

BODY WEIGHT
Record your weight on a balance-type medical scale. Strip down to your bare essentials and be consistent with what you wear. Weigh yourself to the nearest quarter pound.

The best time to weigh yourself is immediately before your workout. You can then record your body weight on your workout sheet above the date.

GET READY FOR GREAT RESULTS!
Before getting started, *read through the rest of this book*. As you look through the 42-day program and study the results that Keith and David achieved, you'll see that some phenomenal gains were made. For example, David gained 25.4 pounds and Keith gained 34.3 pounds . . . in only six weeks. In circumference measurements, each added an average of

- 3 inches in his upper arms
- 4¾ inches on his chest
- 4 inches on his thighs
- 1¾ inches on his calves

While you may not register the same degree of results, your gains should be great—as great as they can be considering your genetics. Follow the program exactly, day-by-day, as it is described and I promise that you won't be disappointed.

Get ready to stimulate your muscles to grow.

Get ready to get bigger—BIGGER MUSCLES in 42 days!

In addition to your lower body workout today, you'll be eating and recording numerous servings of fruits and vegetables. Be sure and purchase plenty of produce from the local supermarket.

DAY 1

SPLIT ROUTINES

By now you should have your measurements taken and your daily calorie expenditure calculated. You should be ready to start the program with a bang!

On the next page you'll notice a listing of Keith Whitley's schedule of everything that he did on Day 1. All his meals and snacks are itemized. I'll continue to do this on the first day of each new week as an example to you of what specific foods that Keith consumed. Blank space under Keith's schedule allows you to follow along and keep track of all your daily activities. This manual, in fact, for the next 42 days will become your workbook or diary. You may want to carry it with you throughout the day.

Keith teaches high school history each weekday during the school year. Locking into a daily schedule not only helps his teaching, but facilitates his bodybuilding. Planning, organizing, and record keeping are key ingredients in successful teaching, bodybuilding, and just about everything of value.

Each of the 42 days will adhere to a similar format. You'll be given an eating plan and a workout (or rest schedule) to follow. You'll be able to benefit from Keith's workout records as well.

Apply this course consistently and you'll have a pattern that will guarantee bigger muscles.

For the first 14 days you'll be training on a three-days-in-a-row, six-days-per-week, split routine. This schedule assumes that Day 1 of the program will fall on a Monday.

For the next three days you'll work three different body parts each day. Here's a brief description of your Day 1 workout, which will be repeated on Day 4, Day 8, and Day 11. More complete exercise descriptions can be found in my previous book *BIG*, on pages 90–119.

1. *Leg curl:* Lift the movement arm slowly to the contracted position in 10 seconds. Pause. Lower smoothly to the bottom in 5 seconds. Repeat for 4 to 8 repetitions.

2. *Leg extension:* Make sure your knees are in line with the rotating axis of the movement arm. Perform as many super-slow repetitions for your quadriceps as possible. Move quickly, without resting, to the leg press.

3. *Leg press:* Adjust your machine, if it is possible, to get maximum range of movement. Keep the repetitions slow and smooth and avoid locking your knees on all but the final repetition. You'll feel the effects of this exercise in your frontal thighs or quadriceps. After the final repetition, get a drink, walk around for several minutes, and prepare for the next leg cycle: leg extension, leg curl, and squat.

4. *Leg extension:* Reduce the resistance by 10 percent for the second set.

5. *Leg curl:* Reduce the weight by 10 percent also. Move immediately from the leg curl to the barbell squat.

6. *Squat with barbell:* The squat performed last in this cycle loads effectively the buttocks and hamstrings. Lift the barbell from the racks and smoothly descend until your hamstrings come in contact with your calves. Take 10 seconds to lift the barbell back almost to the top position. Do not lock your knees. Keep a bend of approximately 15 degrees in your knees. Repeat for maximum repetitions. Rest another minute or two before working your calves.

7. *Donkey calf raise:* Be sure and keep your knees locked as you slowly contract and stretch your calf muscles. Move quickly to the seated calf raise.

8. *Seated calf raise:* The seated calf raise involves the soleus muscle, which lies underneath the gastrocnemius. With a barbell or resistance arm across your knees, do the maximum number of repetitions slowly and smoothly.

9. *Hanging leg raise:* Hang from an overhead bar. Bring your feet up slowly and touch your toes to the bar. Smoothly lower and repeat.

10. *Trunk curl:* Lie on your back. Bring your heels up close to your buttocks. Keep your knees wide. Curl your shoulders slowly in 10 seconds toward your hips. Only one-third of a standard sit-up can be performed in this manner. You'll feel a real burn in your abdominals, especially if you do the exercise immediately after the hanging leg raise.

11. *Back raise:* Lie facedown on a back raise machine, or have a friend hold your legs down securely as you hang your torso over the edge of the high bench. Raise your torso backward slowly and carefully arch your back. Pause. Lower smoothly and repeat.

12. *Stiff-legged deadlift with barbell:* Stand carefully with a barbell. Lower it smoothly down your thighs as far as comfortably possible. Keep a slight bend in your knees. Lift the barbell back to standing position, and repeat. You'll feel a deep burn in your lower back muscles.

Note: A thicker horizontal line in the workout chart indicates a brief rest period. Exercises enclosed by the darker lines compose a body part cycle and should be performed with minimum rest between them.

DAY 1 RECORD

KEITH'S SCHEDULE

6:00am	Wake up!
6:15am	Eat Meal 1.
6:30am	Read newspaper.
7:00am	Get ready for school.
7:30am	Leave for school.
9:00am	Eat Meal 2.
12:00	Eat Meal 3.
3:00pm	Leave school. Return home.
3:30pm	Eat Meal 4.
4:00pm	Relax or take nap.
5:00pm	Leave for gym.
5:30pm	Workout.
6:30pm	Return home.
7:00pm	Eat Meal 5.
7:30pm	Read, study, prepare for next day.
10:00pm	Eat Meal 6.
10:30pm	Bedtime.

YOUR SCHEDULE

KEITH'S CALORIES

MEAL 1: BREAKFAST

3 ounces oatmeal (instant)	300
1 tablespoon margarine	100
4 teaspoons brown sugar	70
2 slices bacon	109
1 cup orange juice	120
1 cup nonfat milk	90

MEAL 2: SNACK

1 plain bagel	200
1 ounce cream cheese	100

MEAL 3: LUNCH

Tuna salad:

1 6½ ounce can tuna in water	200
1 tablespoon mayonnaise	100
2 eggs, boiled & diced	160
1 sliced tomato	35
Relish	10
Combine all on three lettuce leaves	10
2 slices bread	160
1 apple	80
1 cup nonfat milk	90
¼ cup raisins	100

MEAL 4: SNACK

½ 1,800-calorie shake	900
2 chocolate chip cookies commercial	100

MEAL 5: DINNER

Spaghetti and meat sauce:

lean ground meat sauteed with desired vegetables: mushrooms, peppers, and onions, spices, 1 cup tomato sauce	402
1 cup of spaghetti, cooked	605
2 tablespoons parmesan cheese	70
9 breadsticks	335
1 teaspoon margarine	35
1 cup carrots (from frozen)	60

MEAL 6: SNACK

½ 1,800-calorie shake	900
2 chocolate chip cookies	100
Total	**5,541**

YOUR CALORIES

WORKOUT THREE-DAY SPLIT:
Legs, Abdominals, Lower Back

EXERCISE	Keith's Wt/Reps	Your Wt/Reps
1 Leg curl	175 / 7	
2 Leg extension	175 / 8	
3 Leg press	315 / 9	
4 Leg extension	160 / 5	
5 Leg curl	160 / 4	
6 Squat with barbell	225 / 8	
7 Donkey calf raise	360 / 9	
8 Seated calf raise	225 / 6	
9 Hanging leg raise	Bdwt. / 8	
10 Trunk curl	Bdwt. / 12	
11 Back raise	Bdwt. / 6	
12 Stiff-legged deadlift with barbell	185 / 8	

DAY 2

SHOULDERS, UPPER BACK, AND CHEST

On Day 2 you'll be working your shoulders, upper back, and chest. There are four pre-exhaustion cycles: two for shoulders, one for upper back, and one for chest. It's important to move quickly from exercise to exercise within a cycle. Here's the how-to of each.

1. *Lateral raise with dumbbells:* Keep your elbows locked as you slowly raise and lower the dumbbells.

2. *Overhead press with barbell:* Press the bar overhead slowly. Do not lock your elbows. Keep them slightly bent. Lower smoothly and repeat.

3. *Bent-over raise with dumbbells:* Bend over until your torso is parallel to the floor. Raise the dumbbells slowly backward until your hands are shoulder level. Keep your elbows straight during the entire movement.

4. *Press behind neck with barbell:* Use your triceps to force your pre-exhausted deltoids to a deeper level of fatigue. Keep the movements slow and smooth.

5. *Bent-armed pullover with barbell:* Lie face up on a sturdy bench with your head barely off the edge. Have a spotter hand you a barbell and place it on your chest. Lower the bar over your face and head and try to touch the floor. Keep your arms bent and pull the bar back over your face to the chest.

6. *Pulldown to chest on lat machine:* With a narrow underhanded grip, pull the bar slowly to your chest. Pause. Lower smoothly and repeat.

7. *Pullover with one dumbbell:* Lie crossways on a bench and hold a dumbbell on one end with both hands. Keep your arms straight as you lower the dumbbell smoothly behind your head. Stretch and raise the dumbbell slowly in 10 seconds.

8. *Pulldown behind neck on lat machine:* With a parallel grip, if possible, pull the bar slowly behind your neck.

9. *Bent-over row with barbell:* With a narrow underhanded grip, pull the barbell slowly near your thighs and touch your waist. Pause. Lower smoothly and repeat. Take several-minute break and get ready to work your chest.

10. *Bench press with barbell:* Do your bench presses slowly and smoothly, and avoid the lock-out position.

11. *Bent-armed fly with dumbbells:* While lying face up on a bench with dumbbells over your chest, lower the dumbbells to your sides in semicircular arcs as low as comfortably possible. Return the dumbbells slowly in 10 seconds along the same arcs to the top position.

12. *Bench press to neck with barbell:* Lower the barbell smoothly in 5 seconds, keeping your elbows wide, and lightly touch the bar to your neck. Press the barbell slowly in 10 seconds back to the top position.

Today, you'll be blasting your shoulders from several different angles.

DAY 2 RECORD

KEITH'S SCHEDULE

6:00am	Wake up!
6:15am	Eat Meal 1.
6:30am	Read newspaper.
7:00am	Get ready for school.
7:30am	Leave for school.
9:00am	Eat Meal 2.
12:00	Eat Meal 3.
3:00pm	Leave school.
	Return home.
3:30pm	Eat Meal 4.
4:00pm	Relax or take nap.
5:00pm	Leave for gym.
5:30pm	Workout.
6:30pm	Return home.
7:00pm	Eat Meal 5.
7:30pm	Read, study, prepare for next day.
10:00pm	Eat Meal 6.
10:30pm	Bedtime.

YOUR SCHEDULE

YOUR CALORIES

WORKOUT
THREE-DAY SPLIT:
Shoulders, Upper Back, Chest

EXERCISE	Keith's Wt/Reps	Your Wt/Reps
1 Lateral raise with dumbbells	$\frac{60}{7}$	
2 Overhead press with barbell	$\frac{160}{6}$	
3 Bent-over raise with dumbbells	$\frac{50}{5}$	
4 Press behind neck with barbell	$\frac{100}{5}$	
5 Bent-armed pullover with barbell	$\frac{155}{4}$	
6 Pulldown to chest on lat machine	$\frac{130}{8}$	
7 Pullover with one dumbbell	$\frac{65}{6}$	
8 Pulldown behind neck on lat machine	$\frac{130}{7}$	
9 Bent-over row with barbell	$\frac{120}{5}$	
10 Bench press with barbell	$\frac{225}{8}$	
11 Bent-armed fly with dumbbells	$\frac{100}{5}$	
12 Bench press to neck with barbell	$\frac{135}{6}$	

The chest cycle will pump your
pectorals to new heights.

DAY 3

UPPER ARMS, FOREARMS, AND NECK

Upper arms, forearms, and neck are the emphasis muscles today. Here's the order of the routine.

1. *Biceps curl with barbell:* Keep your elbows stable as you curl the barbell slowly. Do as many super-slow repetitions as possible. Immediately go to the dumbbell curl.

2. *Biceps curl with dumbbells:* Curl both dumbbells slowly in 10 seconds while simultaneously turning your hands upward and outward. After maximum repetitions, move to the negative chin-up.

3. *Negative chin-up:* On this exercise you'll use your latissimus dorsi muscles to force your biceps to work even harder. Climb to the top position of the chin-up. Hold steady at the top, remove your feet from the steps, and slowly lower to the stretch in 10 seconds. Climb back and repeat for maximum repetitions.

4. *Triceps extension with one dumbbell:* Hold a dumbbell at one end with both hands and press it overhead. Keep your elbows close to your ears. Bend your elbows and lower the dumbbell behind your neck. Extend the dumbbell slowly back to the top and repeat.

5. *Triceps pressdown on lat machine:* Press the bar downward until your arms are straight. Keep your elbows by your sides. Only your hands and forearms should move. Do as many super-slow repetitions as possible in good form. Immediately move to the dip bars.

6. *Negative dip:* Climb to the top position. Bend your arms and lower your body slowly in 10 seconds. Climb back to the top and repeat. Your triceps should be burning intensely after this exercise.

7. *Wrist curl with barbell:* Grasp the barbell with your palms up and be seated. Rest your forearms on your thighs and the backs of your hands against your knees. Flex and extend your wrists slowly and smoothly.

8. *Reverse wrist curl with barbell:* Use the same position as the wrist curl, except turn your palms down. You'll feel this exercise on the top part of your forearms.

9. *Reverse curl with barbell:* Curl the barbell slowly with a palms-down grip. Practice strict form and your forearms will be stimulated to grow rapidly.

10. *4-way neck machine:* The Nautilus neck machine is ideal for this exercise. Start with the back neck extension. Then go to the front and side to side.

11. *Shoulder shrug with barbell:* Stand with a heavy barbell. Shrug your shoulders slowly and try to touch your ears with your shoulders. Keep your arms straight on both the raising and lowering.

12. *Reverse shoulder shrug:* Mount the parallel bars and straighten your arms. Let your feet drop as low as possible while keeping your arms straight. Then try to lift your torso and put your head on the ceiling. Again, do not bend your arms.

Look down at your hands, and curl the bar slowly in 10 seconds.

DAY 3 RECORD

KEITH'S SCHEDULE

6:00am	Wake up!
6:15am	Eat Meal 1.
6:30am	Read newspaper.
7:00am	Get ready for school.
7:30am	Leave for school.
9:00am	Eat Meal 2.
12:00	Eat Meal 3.
3:00pm	Leave school.
	Return home.
3:30pm	Eat Meal 4.
4:00pm	Relax or take nap.
5:00pm	Leave for gym.
5:30pm	Workout.
6:30pm	Return home.
7:00pm	Eat Meal 5.
7:30pm	Read, study, prepare for next day.
10:00pm	Eat Meal 6.
10:30pm	Bedtime.

YOUR SCHEDULE

YOUR CALORIES

WORKOUT
THREE-DAY SPLIT:
Upper Arms, Forearms, Neck

EXERCISE	Keith's Wt/Reps	Your Wt/Reps
1 Biceps curl with barbell	85/10	
2 Biceps curl with dumbbells	60/6	
3 Negative chin-up	Bdwt. 7	
4 Triceps extension with one dumbbell	50/12	
5 Triceps pressdown on lat machine	50/10	
6 Negative dip	Bdwt. 8	
7 Wrist curl with barbell	75/8	
8 Reverse wrist curl with barbell	40/6	
9 Reverse curl with barbell	40/5	
10 4-way neck machine	30/6	
11 Shoulder shrug with barbell	160/10	
12 Reverse shoulder shrug	Bdwt. 8	

40

Stabilize your elbows during
the triceps pressdown.

WHY SUPER SLOW IS EFFECTIVE

After the first three days you should be sore, pleasantly sore. Most of this soreness should disappear over the next few days since you'll be repeating the routines in the same order.

You should also be catching on to the eating plan. Perhaps you've already added several pounds of body weight. Keep eating those calories and adhering to those super-slow repetitions and your body is sure to grow.

Believing in the super-slow style takes a little patience, especially since you've probably had to reduce the weight initially to learn the form. Here are six reasons why super slow is more effective and efficient than faster styles of lifting and lowering.

- *More muscle tension:* Slow repetitions produce a longer period of effective muscle tension. Faster repetitions employ more momentum and less tension or effort.
- *More muscle force:* Isokinetic evaluations of maximum strength consistently reveal that more muscle force is generated at slower movement speeds. Because of this, fast repetitions are counterproductive for maximum strength development.
- *More muscle fibers:* Muscle force can be increased by activating more muscle fibers or by speeding up the firing rate. Because the firing rate at slow speeds does not exceed the firing rate at fast speeds, the greater muscle force produced at slow speeds is apparently due to greater recruitment of muscle fiber.
- *More muscle power:* Power is the product of force times speed. Power can be enhanced by increasing muscle force, the movement speed, or both. Each component, however, must be trained separately for optimum results. Combining strength training with speed training is not an effective method for improving either the strength factor or the speed factor. You can lift heavy weights slowly or light weights quickly. Because near maximum resistance is essential for maximum strength development, it is recommended that you train with relatively heavy weights and slow speeds to enhance the force factor. As more muscle strength is developed, the force factor increases and permits greater power production.
- *Less tissue trauma:* Slow lifting movements accomplish the same amount of work and produce greater muscle tension than fast lifting movements. But slow weight training causes less tissue trauma at the start and finish of the exercise movements and is less likely to cause injuries. Slow repetitions should be the preferred technique for building muscle.
- *Less momentum:* Momentum plays a part in virtually all forms of exercise. The faster the movement, the greater the momentum. This is an important consideration because as the momentum component increases, the muscle component decreases. Momentum-assisted exercise gives the appearance of greater muscle strength but actually decreases demands on the target muscle groups and increases stress on the joints.

For best results from super-slow exercise, have a training partner push you through the workouts. Here, Keith talks Betsy Hoffmann through a set of curls.

DAY 4 RECORD

KEITH'S SCHEDULE

6:00am	Wake up!
6:15am	Eat Meal 1.
6:30am	Read newspaper.
7:00am	Get ready for school.
7:30am	Leave for school.
9:00am	Eat Meal 2.
12:00	Eat Meal 3.
3:00pm	Leave school. Return home.
3:30pm	Eat Meal 4.
4:00pm	Relax or take nap.
5:00pm	Leave for gym.
5:30pm	Workout.
6:30pm	Return home.
7:00pm	Eat Meal 5.
7:30pm	Read, study, prepare for next day.
10:00pm	Eat Meal 6.
10:30pm	Bedtime.

YOUR SCHEDULE

YOUR CALORIES

WORKOUT
THREE-DAY SPLIT:
Legs, Abdominals, Lower Back

EXERCISE	Keith's Wt/Reps	Your Wt/Reps
1 Leg curl	$\frac{180}{6}$	
2 Leg extensions	$\frac{190}{9}$	
3 Leg press	$\frac{315}{10}$	
4 Leg extension	$\frac{160}{6}$	
5 Leg curl	$\frac{160}{8}$	
6 Squat with barbell	$\frac{235}{9}$	
7 Donkey calf raise	$\frac{380}{8}$	
8 Seated calf raise	$\frac{225}{7}$	
9 Hanging leg raise	$\frac{Bdwt.}{10}$	
10 Trunk curl	$\frac{Bdwt.+15}{7}$	
11 Back raise	$\frac{Bdwt.}{9}$	
12 Stiff-legged deadlift with barbell	$\frac{185}{9}$	

44

On most weekday mornings, Keith would prepare his breakfast, lunch, and snacks, place them in plastic containers, and carry them to school for eating throughout the day.

PROPER BREATHING

One of the real challenges in using super slow, especially when heavier, more intense work is done, is the feeling that you're not getting enough air. You are probably holding your breath, taking a deep breath, holding your breath, taking a deep breath, and so on. In other words you are off/on-ing your breathing.

Many times such off/on-ing is synced to jerking or moving the weight too fast. Actually, what is desired is the exact opposite: continuous, relaxed ventilation combined with a steady contraction force.

Try not to hold your breath during any super-slow repetition. Keep your mouth open, relax your face and neck, and breathe—breathe—breathe.

Deep breaths are not necessary. In fact, it's to your benefit to practice short, rapid breaths with emphasis on blowing out rather than taking in large gulps of air. Try to ventilate just enough so your breathing never stops.

Doing so will reduce the tendency that you may have to get dizzy or develop a headache. It will also increase the loading of the muscle, which will lead to greater growth stimulation.

Emphasize short, rapid breathing out during your training session today and see if it doesn't lead to the performance of at least one more repetition in each exercise.

Emphasize breathing out during each super-slow repetition and try not to hold your breath.

DAY 5 RECORD

KEITH'S SCHEDULE

6:00am	Wake up!
6:15am	Eat Meal 1.
6:30am	Read newspaper.
7:00am	Get ready for school.
7:30am	Leave for school.
9:00am	Eat Meal 2.
12:00	Eat Meal 3.
3:00pm	Leave school.
	Return home.
3:30pm	Eat Meal 4.
4:00pm	Relax or take nap.
5:00pm	Leave for gym.
5:30pm	Workout.
6:30pm	Return home.
7:00pm	Eat Meal 5.
7:30pm	Attend sporting event.
10:00pm	Return home.
10:30pm	Eat Meal 6.
11:00pm	Bedtime.

YOUR SCHEDULE

YOUR CALORIES

WORKOUT THREE-DAY SPLIT:
Shoulders, Upper Back, Chest

EXERCISE	Keith's Wt/Reps	Your Wt/Reps
1 Lateral raise with dumbbells	$\frac{60}{8}$	
2 Overhead press with barbell	$\frac{160}{8}$	
3 Bent-over raise with dumbbells	$\frac{50}{6}$	
4 Press behind neck with barbell	$\frac{100}{6}$	
5 Bent-armed pullover with barbell	$\frac{155}{6}$	
6 Pulldown to chest on lat machine	$\frac{140}{7}$	
7 Pullover with one dumbbell	$\frac{65}{7}$	
8 Pulldown behind neck on lat machine	$\frac{130}{9}$	
9 Bent-over row with barbell	$\frac{120}{7}$	
10 Bench press with barbell	$\frac{230}{7}$	
11 Bent-armed fly with dumbbells	$\frac{100}{6}$	
12 Bench press to neck with barbell	$\frac{145}{6}$	

Contrary to what you read in the muscle magazines, vitamin and mineral pills are *not* necessary for optimum bodybuilding. You can get all the essential vitamins and minerals from a mixed diet, such as that recommended in this book.

THE ALMOST PERFECT EXERCISE

The wrist curl with a barbell, if performed in the correct manner, is almost a perfect exercise. It provides full-range directness of resistance and varying resistance that almost matches your potential strength.

To begin with, the resistance in the wrist curl is applied directly to your primary moving body part, the hands. Second, the arc of movement is such that the resistance increases as the work is performed. If the angle of the forearm on your thighs is proper, the resistance reaches its highest point just as the involved muscles reach their strongest positions. Third, the geometry of the involved joints and muscular attachments is such that the strength curve progresses throughout the movement, steadily increasing as the muscles shorten from full stretch to full contraction.

For maximum results, do the wrist curl as follows: (1) Grasp the barbell with a medium, palms-up grip. (2) Sit with your hips higher than your knees. (3) Place your elbows and forearms securely on your thighs and make certain your elbows are higher than your wrists. In other words, your forearms should be in a declined position. (4) Lean forward with your upper body until the angle between your biceps and forearms is less than 90 degrees. (5) Flex your wrists slowly. (6) Pause in the contracted position. (7) Lower smoothly and repeat. (8) Do not allow your fingers to unroll. Keep the barbell firmly in the palms of your hands.

Most bodybuilders cheat in the wrist curl by moving their elbows down and up, which shortens the range of movement and decreases the growth stimulation. They also lean their torsos backward and start moving their heels, which brings into action other muscles. The isolation of the forearms is reduced as a result and the effect on the targeted muscles is much less.

Don't allow this to happen in your training. Stick with correct form and your forearms will grow at a much faster rate.

You can do the wrist curl with your forearms on your thighs, or on a bench as shown. In either style, keep the angle between your upper arms and forearms at less than 90 degrees.

DAY 6

DAY 6 RECORD

KEITH'S SCHEDULE

7:00am	Wake up!
7:15am	Eat Meal 1.
7:30am	Read newspaper.
8:00am	Do home chores.
10:00am	Eat Meal 2.
10:30am	Wash cars.
12:00	Eat Meal 3.
12:30pm	Go grocery shopping.
3:00pm	Return home.
3:15pm	Eat Meal 4.
5:00pm	Leave for workout.
5:30pm	Workout.
6:30pm	Return home.
7:00pm	Eat Meal 5.
7:30pm	Go to movie.
11:00pm	Return home.
11:15pm	Eat Meal 6.
11:30pm	Bedtime.

YOUR SCHEDULE

YOUR CALORIES

WORKOUT
THREE-DAY SPLIT:
Upper Arms, Forearms, Neck

EXERCISE	Keith's Wt/Reps	Your Wt/Reps
1 Biceps curl with barbell	90/8	
2 Biceps curl with dumbbells	60/7	
3 Negative chin-up	Bdwt./4	
4 Triceps extension with one dumbbell	60/8	
5 Triceps pressdown on lat machine	60/8	
6 Negative dip	Bdwt./9	
7 Wrist curl with barbell	75/10	
8 Reverse wrist curl with barbell	45/8	
9 Reverse curl with barbell	40/6	
10 4-way neck machine	30/8	
11 Shoulder shrug with barbell	170/10	
12 Reverse shoulder shrug	Bdwt.+10/10	

On the negative chin-up, take a full 10 seconds to lower your body from the top to the bottom.

RECOVERY ABILITY

Today is an off-day. You should be getting lots of rest and lots of food and drink. After six consecutive days of training, you need to concentrate on replenishing your recovery ability.

Recovery ability is defined as the chemical reactions that are necessary for your body to produce muscular growth. An optimum recovery ability is dependent on adequate rest, balanced nutrition, and time.

Muscular size and strength occur ordinarily as part of normal growth. Little exercise is required for reaching normal development. As a bodybuilder, however, you seek abnormal levels. Your objective is to build maximum levels of muscular size in the shortest time from the least effort. It only follows that you should be looking for the most productive method of exercise.

A healthy body will provide levels of size and strength according to its perception of what is needed for normal requirements, plus a bit more as a reserve for emergency use. As long as existing levels are adequate, as long as extreme demands are not made on the body, no additional size or strength will be provided. To produce growth, demands must be made in excess of normal. Only then will the body attempt to provide the size and strength required to meet these demands if it can. Note the phrase *if it can*.

Your body is a complex factory, constantly making hundreds of delicate changes that transform food and oxygen into many chemicals needed by various parts of the system. But there is a limit to the chemical conversions that your recovery ability can make within a given time. If your requirements exceed that limit, your body will eventually be overworked to the point of collapse.

The recovery ability of your body provides normal growth. It also provides abnormal growth, if such abnormal growth is dictated, and if the recovery ability is able to meet the requirements. It is not possible for you to exhaust your recovery ability while doing nothing to stimulate abnormal growth.

DAY 7

Obviously, then, to be productive, an exercise must stimulate abnormal growth as much as possible while disturbing the recovery ability as little as possible. Under this concept an ideal exercise would be infinitely hard and infinitely brief. It would provide maximum growth stimulation while leaving your recovery ability in the best possible shape to meet the requirements for growth.

Take advantage of your off-day and the subsequent off-days as they occur on a more frequent basis. The right amount of rest, relaxation, and time are necessary for getting bigger.

Relax, grab a good book, and get plenty of rest today.

DAY 7 RECORD

KEITH'S SCHEDULE

8:00am	Wake up!
8:15am	Eat Meal 1.
8:30am	Read newspaper.
10:00am	Eat Meal 2.
10:30am	Attend church.
12:30pm	Eat buffet brunch, Meals 3 & 4.
1:30pm	Return home.
2:00pm	Watch TV.
4:00pm	Take a nap.
5:30pm	Enjoy drive or walk.
7:00pm	Eat Meal 5.
7:30pm	Relax or prepare for next day.
10:00pm	Eat Meal 6.
10:30pm	Bedtime.

YOUR SCHEDULE

YOUR CALORIES

KEITH'S FAVORITES

These recipes appear throughout the book on the DAY RECORD pages. The recipes do not necessarily relate to the pages on which they appear.

SIRLOIN BURGER

- ¾ pound lean ground sirloin
- 2 ounces aged Swiss cheese, grated
- ¼ cup fresh mushrooms, chopped
- 1 tablespoon onion, finely chopped
- ⅛ teaspoon liquid smoke

Combine all ingredients and mix well. Form patties 1-inch thick and broil several minutes on each side (medium rare).

Yield: 2 servings
Calories 405/serving

BRAWNY BURGER

- ⅔ pound lean ground sirloin
- 2 ounces Braunschweiger (liver sausage)
- 1 tablespoon plain nonfat yogurt
- 2 tablespoons onion, finely minced
- 1 teaspoon caraway seeds

Combine all ingredients and mix well. Form patties 1-inch thick and broil several minutes on each side (medium rare).

Yield: 2 servings
Calories: 365/serving

CORN CASSEROLE

- 2 cups skim milk
- 1 onion, medium, chopped
- 2 red or green peppers, chopped
- 2 eggs
- 2 teaspoons butter-flavored salt
  Pinch of pepper

Scald the milk. Stir in remaining ingredients and turn mixture into a casserole. Bake in a preheated 325°F oven for about 1¼ hours.

Yield: 8 servings
Calories: 89/serving

Remember to keep your calories at a high level. Several recommended blender drinks are listed on page 132.

DAY 8

VALUE OF PRE-EXHAUSTION

It will be to your advantage during the second week, and subsequent weeks, of this program to concentrate on moving very quickly from one exercise to the next during each body part cycle.

Moving quickly, in less than three seconds, from a single-joint exercise to a multiple-joint exercise, is called pre-exhaustion. Pre-exhaustion makes it possible to work almost any large muscle harder than would normally be possible.

In exercises involving two or more muscles and joints, a point of failure is reached when the weakest muscle is no longer able to continue. In this case little growth stimulation is provided for the stronger muscle involved in the same exercise.

In the barbell squat, for example, failure is usually reached when the lower back muscles fatigue. This happens before the stronger hamstrings and quadriceps of the thighs have been worked as hard as necessary to produce the best possible results. But by pre-exhausting the thigh muscles the problem can be solved.

First, do the leg extensions in the super-slow style for maximum repetitions. Second, do the leg curl in the same manner. Third, do the barbell squat, but allow no rest following the leg curl, not even for a second or two. Run immediately to the squat racks and start squatting.

You will find that very little resistance is required for the squats, probably less than half the amount of weight that you normally use. Regardless of the light weight being used, when you do reach a point of failure in your squats, it will not be because your lower back fatigued before your thighs were worked properly. When you fail, it will be because your thighs are exhausted. And your thighs will be worked far harder than previously.

By pre-exhausting your thighs before squatting, you have removed the weak link represented by lower-back involvement in squats.

Other examples of pre-exhaustion that are applied during this week or other weeks are: trunk curl followed by hanging leg raise, back raise followed by stiff-legged deadlift, and lateral raise followed by overhead press. In these cases the single-joint exercise precedes the multiple-joint movement. Sometimes two or more single-joint movements are stacked before the final exercise, which make the cycle even harder.

In all cycles, however, keep the time between exercises to three seconds or less. Thus, you may need to rearrange your equipment according. Once you understand pre-exhaustion, you can use it to enormous advantage in almost every workout.

In working your legs in the recommended pre-exhaustion style, it is important to have the leg extension close to the leg press, and the leg curl close to the squat bar.

DAY 8 RECORD

KEITH'S SCHEDULE

6:00am	Wake up!
6:15am	Eat Meal 1.
6:30am	Read newspaper.
7:00am	Get ready for school.
7:30am	Leave for school.
9:00am	Eat Meal 2.
12:00	Eat Meal 3.
3:00pm	Leave school. Return home.
3:30pm	Eat Meal 4.
4:00pm	Relax or take nap.
5:00pm	Leave for gym.
5:30pm	Workout.
6:30pm	Return home.
7:00pm	Eat Meal 5.
7:30pm	Read, study, prepare for next day.
10:00pm	Eat Meal 6.
10:30pm	Bedtime.

YOUR SCHEDULE

KEITH'S CALORIES

MEAL 1: BREAKFAST

2 eggs any style	160
2 English muffins, toasted	280
3 tablespoons jelly/preserves	150
½ cantaloupe	50
1 cup nonfat milk	90

MEAL 2: SNACK

Cheese sandwich:	
2 slices bread	160
2 ounces cheese	200
½ cup applesauce	50

MEAL 3: LUNCH

4 slices bread	320
8 slices turkey	280
1 cup cream cottage cheese	235
1 cup canned orange sections	130
2 whole carrots	65
1 cup nonfat milk	150

MEAL 4: SNACK

½ 2,000-calorie shake	1,000
4 chocolate chip cookies	200

MEAL 5: DINNER

2 cups chili with beans & beef	680
1 cup cooked brown rice	235
2 cups chopped broccoli	100
2 cornbread muffins	290
1 cup nonfat milk	100

MEAL 6: SNACK

½ 2,000-calorie shake	1,000
4 chocolate chip cookies	200
Total	6,055

YOUR CALORIES

WORKOUT THREE-DAY SPLIT:
Legs, Abdominals, Lower Back

EXERCISE	Keith's Wt/Reps	Your Wt/Reps
1 Leg curl	$\frac{185}{5}$	
2 Leg extension	$\frac{205}{6}$	
3 Leg press	$\frac{340}{8}$	
4 Leg extension	$\frac{165}{6}$	
5 Leg curl	$\frac{165}{6}$	
6 Squat with barbell	$\frac{245}{8}$	
7 Donkey calf raise	$\frac{380}{9}$	
8 Seated calf raise	$\frac{225}{8}$	
9 Hanging leg raise	$\frac{\text{Bdwt.}}{10}$	
10 Trunk curl	$\frac{\text{Bdwt.}+15}{15}$	
11 Back raise	$\frac{\text{Bdwt.}}{12}$	
12 Stiff-legged deadlift with barbell	$\frac{190}{9}$	

Another pre-exhaustion cycle for the chest involves the cable crossover immediately followed by the dip.

DAY 9

BUILD STRENGTH, NOT DEMONSTRATE IT

A workout is one thing; a competitive weightlifting contest is a different matter. The best way to *build* strength has little in common with the best way to *demonstrate* strength. Yet many bodybuilders make the mistake of training as if they were in a weightlifting meet, perhaps being more interested in impressing their peers than in trying to build muscular size and strength.

Olympic lifters and power lifters must practice maximum, single-attempt lifts, both in training and in competition. But there is no reason for bodybuilders ever to attempt heavy singles. While maximum muscular size cannot be produced without maximum muscular strength, it does not follow that building strength requires heavy single-attempt lifts. On the contrary, greater strength and size will result from the performance of super-slow repetitions within the 4 to 8 range.

Maximum size and strength can be produced without ever exerting maximum force, even though maximum contraction force is a requirement for maximum growth stimulation. For growth stimulation, it is only necessary to produce momentary maximum contraction force. This can and should be done only after your momentary ability has been reduced by the performance of at least three repetitions that did not involve maximum contraction force. In effect, by the time you produce maximum force, your momentary ability will be reduced to the point at which the danger of injury is greatly decreased.

Bodybuilders do not hurt themselves during a first repetition because they were not warmed up properly. They hurt themselves because they are strongest at that point in the set. And they make the mistake of moving at maximum speed at a time when this results in more pull and much more jerk from the geometrical increase in the acceleration factor. Since single-attempt lifts are always first repetitions, it should be evident that they are the most dangerous type of movements.

Since maximum growth stimulation can be induced by momentary maximum contraction force, most of the potential danger can be avoided by reducing the existing level of ability before producing maximum force. Once again, you can accomplish this by performing three or four repetitions immediately prior to a maximum movement. Or it can be even better accomplished by pre-exhausting the muscles by working them in an isolated fashion immediately prior to involving them in a heavier multiple-joint movement.

The performance of full squats is equally important for weightlifters and bodybuilders.

DAY 9 RECORD

KEITH'S SCHEDULE

6:00am	Wake up!
6:15am	Eat Meal 1.
6:30am	Read newspaper.
7:00am	Get ready for school.
7:30am	Leave for school.
9:00am	Eat Meal 2.
12:00	Eat Meal 3.
3:00pm	Leave school.
	Return home.
3:30pm	Eat Meal 4.
4:00pm	Relax or take nap.
5:00pm	Leave for gym.
5:30pm	Workout.
6:30pm	Return home.
7:00pm	Eat Meal 5.
7:30pm	Read, study, prepare for next day.
10:00pm	Eat Meal 6.
10:30pm	Bedtime.

YOUR SCHEDULE

YOUR CALORIES

WORKOUT THREE-DAY SPLIT:
Shoulders, Upper Back, Chest

EXERCISE	Keith's Wt/Reps	Your Wt/Reps
1 Lateral raise with dumbbells	60/9	
2 Overhead press with barbell	170/6	
3 Bent-over raise with dumbbells	50/7	
4 Press behind neck with barbell	100/8	
5 Bent-armed pullover with barbell	155/8	
6 Pulldown to chest on lat machine	140/7	
7 Pullover with one dumbbell	65/8	
8 Pulldown behind neck on lat machine	140/7	
9 Bent-over row with barbell	130/4	
10 Bench press with barbell	235/7	
11 Bent-armed fly with dumbbells	100/7	
12 Bench press to neck with barbell	145/7	

CARROTS IN ORANGE JUICE

1 pound carrots, sliced on the diagonal into ⅓-inch-thick ovals
½ cup orange juice

Put carrots in a small sauce pan or casserole with a tight cover. Add the orange juice. Cover and either simmer on top of the stove about 20 minutes or bake in the oven for 30 minutes.

Yield: 3 servings
Calories: 75/serving

Citrus fruits should be consumed daily by all bodybuilders.

THE MOST DANGEROUS REPETITION

DAY 10

Most bodybuilders believe that they are avoiding injury if they terminate a set prior to the most difficult repetitions. They consider the last repetitions the most dangerous. In fact, the opposite is true. The farther you progress into a set, the safer the work.

Regardless of the number of repetitions involved in a set, the first repetition is the most dangerous and the last repetition is the safest. The more difficult it feels, the safer it is. The more dangerous it seems, the safer it is.

The last of 8 repetitions, for example, feels harder to do because you are almost exhausted by the time you reach that point in the set. You do not feel your actual output; instead you feel the percentage of your momentarily possible output. If you can press 200 pounds, then 100 pounds will feel light to you during the first repetition and will feel heavier during each following repetition. By the time you reach a point at which you are capable of performing one more repetition, the 100 pounds will feel very heavy. At that moment the 100 pounds you are lifting will actually be very heavy, since it will momentarily require 100 percent of your strength to move it.

Everything is relative insofar as feelings are concerned. The danger of injury, however, is not related directly to those feelings. Instead, your connective tissues have an actual level of resistance to pull, and since they do not perform work in the sense that they do not contract like muscles, their resistance is not reduced during the performance of a set of several repetitions. If a particular tendon has an existing level of resistance capable of withstanding 100 units of pull, then that level of resistance remains constant throughout a set. It will be 100 units during the first repetition and 100 units during the eighth repetition. Yet the danger factor changes. During the first repetition you might be momentarily capable of exerting 200 units of pull. If you do so, then an injury will surely result. By the time you reach the eighth repetition, however, your momentary ability may be reduced to only 10 units of pull. At that point you are not strong enough to hurt yourself.

Unfortunately, most bodybuilders avoid the most productive repetitions in all their sets because of an unjustified fear of injury. After working right up to the point at which one more repetition would have done some good, they stop. They are actually avoiding the safest repetition of all, the only one capable of producing the maximum growth stimulation they seek.

Don't let this happen in your training. Always work through those last repetitions.

Bodybuilders often neglect their neck muscles. If you have access to a 4-way neck machine, use it regularly. If not, use a neck harness.

DAY 10 RECORD

KEITH'S SCHEDULE

6:00am	Wake up!
6:15am	Eat Meal 1.
6:30am	Read newspaper.
7:00am	Get ready for school.
7:30am	Leave for school.
9:00am	Eat Meal 2.
12:00	Eat Meal 3.
3:00pm	Leave school.
	Return home.
3:30pm	Eat Meal 4.
4:00pm	Relax or take nap.
5:00pm	Leave for gym.
5:30pm	Workout.
6:30pm	Return home.
7:00pm	Eat Meal 5.
7:30pm	Read, study, prepare for next day.
10:00pm	Eat Meal 6.
10:30pm	Bedtime.

YOUR SCHEDULE

YOUR CALORIES

WORKOUT
THREE-DAY SPLIT:
Upper Arms, Forearms, Neck

EXERCISE	Keith's Wt/Reps	Your Wt/Reps
1 Biceps curl with barbell	$\frac{95}{9}$	
2 Biceps curl with dumbbells	$\frac{65}{5}$	
3 Negative chin-up	$\frac{Bdwt.}{5}$	
4 Triceps extension with one dumbbell	$\frac{65}{11}$	
5 Triceps pressdown on lat machine	$\frac{65}{5}$	
6 Negative dip	$\frac{Bdwt.+20}{8}$	
7 Wrist curl with barbell	$\frac{80}{8}$	
8 Reverse wrist curl with barbell	$\frac{50}{7}$	
9 Reverse curl with barbell	$\frac{40}{8}$	
10 4-way neck machine	$\frac{35}{7}$	
11 Shoulder shrug with barbell	$\frac{180}{9}$	
12 Reverse shoulder shrug	$\frac{Bdwt.+20}{8}$	

TUNA MACARONI TOSS

- 3 cups elbow macaroni cooked according to directions on package
- 2 7-ounce cans water-packed tuna
- ½ cup green pepper strips
- ¼ cup thinly sliced green onion
- 2 tablespoons dried pimiento
- ½ cup diet French dressing

Combine all ingredients and toss well.

Yield: 6 servings
Calories: 168/serving

The reverse curl stresses your gripping and forearm extensor muscles.

SUPER-SLOW TECHNIQUES

Pretend that you are performing leg extension. You complete four repetitions and begin a fifth.

You sense that your speed is bogging down. You remain determined to maintain uniform speed. However, the speed grows slower as you become weaker.

Realize that as your musculature becomes weaker, it becomes feeble. Often it can still lift the movement arm, but only very slowly. Such slow movement and muscle feebleness dull sense of position and movement.

Even though you are moving, you do not perceive it. You must actively sense or feel to detect movement.

Deliberately refuse to accept the idea that you are no longer moving. Believe in it. Have the mind-set that even though the muscle is incapable, *I'm going to complete the movement anyway!*

In many cases, upward movement will continue and you'll complete the repetition. *Give it time. Whittle on it.* The repetition may require 30 seconds to finish.

Once the repetition completes, smoothly lower it and try another.

Never, never give up if additional positive movement is possible. And then stop only after you've spent another 10 to 15 seconds trying for an extra fraction of an inch.

These helpful hints above were paraphrased from Ken Hutchins' revised book, *Super Slow: The Ultimate Exercise Protocol,* which I highly recommend. Ken has supervised over 10,000 super-slow workouts, and no one understands the philosophy and techniques better than he does.

To order a copy of this technical manual, send a check or money order for $26.50 to Media Support, P.O. Box 180154, Casselberry, FL 32718-0154.

Occasionally it's okay to have an assistant help you do several forced repetitions at the end of a super-slow set.

On any large-muscle exercise, such as the deadlift, pay special attention to keeping your face relaxed.

DAY 11 RECORD

KEITH'S SCHEDULE

6:00am	Wake up!
6:15am	Eat Meal 1.
6:30am	Read newspaper.
7:00am	Get ready for school.
7:30am	Leave for school.
9:00am	Eat Meal 2.
12:00	Eat Meal 3.
3:00pm	Leave school.
	Return home.
3:30pm	Eat Meal 4.
4:00pm	Relax or take nap.
5:00pm	Leave for gym.
5:30pm	Workout.
6:30pm	Return home.
7:00pm	Eat Meal 5.
7:30pm	Read, study, prepare for next day.
10:00pm	Eat Meal 6.
10:30pm	Bedtime.

YOUR SCHEDULE

YOUR CALORIES

WORKOUT
THREE-DAY SPLIT:
Legs, Abdominals, Lower Back

EXERCISE	Keith's Wt/Reps	Your Wt/Reps
1 Leg curl	$\frac{190}{4}$	
2 Leg extension	$\frac{210}{7}$	
3 Leg press	$\frac{360}{9}$	
4 Leg extension	$\frac{170}{7}$	
5 Leg curl	$\frac{170}{6}$	
6 Squat with barbell	$\frac{255}{10}$	
7 Donkey calf raise	$\frac{400}{11}$	
8 Seated calf raise	$\frac{225}{10}$	
9 Hanging leg raise	$\frac{Bdwt.}{11}$	
10 Trunk curl	$\frac{Bdwt.+20}{9}$	
11 Back raise	$\frac{Bdwt.+10}{9}$	
12 Stiff-legged deadlift with barbell	$\frac{195}{9}$	

After a week of high-intensity, super-slow training, you should not feel worn out, but invigorated.

DAY 12

SHORT AND INFREQUENT WORKOUTS

Proper exercise increases strength by creating a need for growth. It makes demands on your body that cannot easily be met by its existing muscular development. If the existing level of strength is adequate for the normal work loads encountered, there is no need for growth. Your body will not provide something that is not required, at least not in the way of muscular size and strength.

Within broad limits, you can do almost anything you want to with a program of proper exercise. The limits of muscular growth are determined by individual potential. But within those limits, striking degrees of physical improvement can be produced in almost anybody.

Producing these improvements does not take years of steady training, nor does it require you to spend half your life in a gym. Quite the contrary is true. Gratifying results can come very quickly from short and infrequent workouts, while continuing many other types of physical activity, and while improving your strength and stamina.

Exercise should constantly improve your strength and increase your overall ability in other physical activities. What frequently happens in practice is a far cry from what should have happened. Instead of producing an ever-increasing feeling of strength and well-being, an improper exercise program will leave you feeling constantly tired, with little energy for anything else.

A persistent tired feeling should be a warning that something is wrong. Unfortunately, it is a warning that is frequently ignored. If you are untrained, you will feel tired as a result of your first few workouts, but this feeling should not continue. If it does, you are overtraining. In short, your workouts are exceeding your recovery ability.

On the other hand, as a bodybuilder, you should be tired at the end of a workout. This is true even though you may have trained for years. But you should not remain tired. Within 20 minutes you should have recovered and feel capable of going through your entire workout again. And you should be able to do so, even though you should never try. It takes very little high-intensity exercise to stimulate growth.

Never do more exercise when you can get better results from less. Strive to make your less exercise harder.

DAY 12 RECORD

KEITH'S SCHEDULE

6:00am	Wake up!
6:15am	Eat Meal 1.
6:30am	Read newspaper.
7:00am	Get ready for school.
7:30am	Leave for school.
9:00am	Eat Meal 2.
12:00	Eat Meal 3.
3:00pm	Leave school.
	Return home.
3:30pm	Eat Meal 4.
4:00pm	Relax or take nap.
5:00pm	Leave for gym.
5:30pm	Workout.
6:30pm	Return home.
7:00pm	Eat Meal 5.
7:30pm	Attend sporting event.
10:00pm	Return home.
10:30pm	Eat Meal 6.
11:00pm	Bedtime.

YOUR SCHEDULE

YOUR CALORIES

WORKOUT
THREE-DAY SPLIT:
Shoulders, Upper Back, Chest

EXERCISE	Keith's Wt/Reps	Your Wt/Reps
1 Lateral raise with dumbbells	$\frac{65}{5}$	
2 Overhead press with barbell	$\frac{170}{7}$	
3 Bent-over raise with dumbbells	$\frac{50}{8}$	
4 Press behind neck with barbell	$\frac{105}{7}$	
5 Bent-armed pullover with barbell	$\frac{160}{6}$	
6 Pulldown to chest on lat machine	$\frac{140}{9}$	
7 Pullover with one dumbbell	$\frac{70}{8}$	
8 Pulldown behind neck on lat machine	$\frac{145}{7}$	
9 Bent-over row with barbell	$\frac{130}{5}$	
10 Bench press with barbell	$\frac{240}{8}$	
11 Bent-armed fly with dumbbells	$\frac{100}{8}$	
12 Bench press to neck with barbell	$\frac{150}{7}$	

With the correct combination of exercise, nutrition, and rest, your muscles should be getting bigger and stronger day by day.

BICEPS ACTION

The prime action of the biceps is supination, or twisting of the hand. On the right arm, the biceps supinates the hand in a clockwise direction; on the left, the twisting is done counterclockwise. The bending action accomplished by the biceps is strictly secondary.

One simple test will prove this: Bend your forearm toward your upper arm as far as possible, while keeping your hand in a pronated position. Place your other hand on your biceps of the bent arm. Note that your biceps is not contracted, even though the bending action has been completed. In other words, though your arm is bent as far as possible, your biceps has only performed part of its function. Now twist the hand of your bent arm into a supinated position and feel your biceps contract. Full contraction of the biceps results in twisting your hand and forearm, and your biceps cannot fully contract unless the twisting occurs.

For this reason, you can curl more in a palms-up position than you can in a palms-down grip. In the reverse curl position, your biceps is prevented from twisting into full contraction; thus it is impossible to involve all the available muscle fibers in the work being performed.

The apparent difference in strength that is so obvious when the normal curl is compared to the reverse curl demonstrates the fact that twisting the forearm increases the bending strength of the arm. It is also true that bending the arm increases the twisting strength. This is illustrated when you twist a dumbbell in various positions. It will be apparent that you can exert a greater twisting force with a bent arm than you can with a straight arm.

From the above discussion it should be plain that using an easy-curl bar to work your biceps is not as effective as using a straight bar. An easy-curl bar moves your hands in the direction of pronation rather than supination. It does not fully pronate your hand, but it goes at least partway, too far to permit your biceps to function best.

Thus, any exercise for the biceps should be done with a fully supinated, palms-up grip.

Curls with a straight bar allow supination of your hands and forearms, which produces a higher involvement of the biceps.

DAY 13 RECORD

KEITH'S SCHEDULE

7:00am	Wake up!
7:15am	Eat Meal 1.
7:30am	Read newspaper.
8:00am	Do home chores.
10:00am	Eat Meal 2.
10:30am	Wash cars.
12:00	Eat Meal 3.
12:30pm	Go grocery shopping.
3:00pm	Return home.
3:15pm	Eat Meal 4.
5:00pm	Leave for workout.
5:30pm	Workout.
6:30pm	Return home.
7:00pm	Eat Meal 5.
7:30pm	Go to movie.
11:00pm	Return home.
11:15pm	Eat Meal 6.
11:30pm	Bedtime.

YOUR SCHEDULE

YOUR CALORIES

WORKOUT THREE-DAY SPLIT:
Upper Arms, Forearms, Neck

EXERCISE	Keith's Wt/Reps	Your Wt/Reps
1 Biceps curl with barbell	$\dfrac{100}{8}$	
2 Biceps curl with dumbbells	$\dfrac{65}{8}$	
3 Negative chin-up	$\dfrac{\text{Bdwt.}}{8}$	
4 Triceps extension with one dumbbell	$\dfrac{70}{10}$	
5 Triceps pressdown on lat machine	$\dfrac{70}{4}$	
6 Negative dip	$\dfrac{\text{Bdwt.}+30}{8}$	
7 Wrist curl with barbell	$\dfrac{85}{10}$	
8 Reverse wrist curl with barbell	$\dfrac{55}{8}$	
9 Reverse curl with barbell	$\dfrac{40}{9}$	
10 4-way neck machine	$\dfrac{40}{6}$	
11 Shoulder shrug with barbell	$\dfrac{200}{10}$	
12 Reverse shoulder shrug	$\dfrac{\text{Bdwt.}+30}{10}$	

Curls with an easy-curl bar move your hands toward pronation, which limits the action of the biceps.

THE STRONGER NEED LESS

While proper exercise is capable of producing enormous increases in muscular mass and strength, it apparently does not produce a proportionate increase in the capability of your recovery ability.

In practice, this means that a stronger person literally cannot stand as much high-intensity work as a weaker person. When regular training is started, a beginner will grow rapidly as a result of high-intensity training, even if he trains three or four times as much as is required. Apparently, a weak individual is unable to exceed the recovery ability of his system. He is not strong enough to impose a demand on his recovery ability that cannot be met. As he becomes stronger he starts making demands on his recovery ability that are difficult to meet. Now, his ability to make such demands is increasing more rapidly than his ability to meet them. Eventually, when a level of greater-than-average strength has been achieved, he becomes capable of making demands that simply cannot be met. At this strength level, the amount of training must be reduced.

After two weeks of six-day-per-week training, your recovery ability has been taxed to the maximum. During the next two weeks, the duration of your workouts will be reduced and the frequency will be decreased.

You should get plenty of rest and relaxation today. Perhaps you'll want to check your food supplies and make a list of the various foods you'll need for weeks 3 and 4. With this list in hand, why not take a drive down to the supermarket? You'll be upping your calories again tomorrow.

For the record, both Keith and David had each put on slightly more than 10 pounds of body weight by the end of day 14. Be sure and keep accurate accounts of your eating, exercising, and body weight.

Eat and rest well today to replenish your recovery ability.

DAY 14 RECORD

KEITH'S SCHEDULE

8:00am	Wake up!
8:15am	Eat Meal 1.
8:30am	Read newspaper.
10:00am	Eat Meal 2.
10:30am	Attend church.
12:30pm	Eat buffet brunch, Meals 3 & 4.
1:30pm	Return home.
2:00pm	Watch TV.
4:00pm	Take a nap.
5:30pm	Enjoy drive or walk.
7:00pm	Eat Meal 5.
7:30pm	Relax or prepare for next day.
10:00pm	Eat Meal 6.
10:30pm	Bedtime.

YOUR SCHEDULE

YOUR CALORIES

SWEET AND SPICY PORK STEW

1½ pounds lean ground pork
1 medium onion, minced
2 cloves fresh garlic, pressed
1 teaspoon dried sage
⅛ teaspoon allspice
¼ teaspoon salt
6 cups Poultry Stock
3 sweet potatoes, peeled and cut into ¾-inch slices
3 ribs celery, cut into 1-inch diagonal pieces
2 large pears, peeled, cored, and cut into 1-inch chunks
1 teaspoon dried savory
¼ teaspoon paprika

Mix pork, onion, garlic, sage, allspice, and salt together well. For meatballs about 1 inch in diameter. In a large kettle or stockpot, slowly cook meatballs to brown them on all sides. Usually ground pork has enough fat in it so that when it begins to cook, no oil is needed. Use the stock as needed for liquid to get it started.

When done, after 10–15 minutes of cooking, drain off any fat, then add remaining stock, sweet potatoes, and celery. Bring stock to a boil, lower heat, and simmer covered for 20 minutes. Add pears, seasonings, and salt to taste if desired. Continue to simmer partially covered for another 10 minutes or until sweet potatoes are tender.

Yield: 8 servings
Calories: 428/serving

DEVILED EGGS

6 eggs
¼ cup plain, low-fat yogurt
1 teaspoon fresh lemon juice
½ teaspoon Worcestershire sauce
¼ teaspoon dry mustard
6 black olives, pitted and sliced

Hard-boil the eggs, peel and slice in half lengthwise. Remove yolks and mash them with remaining ingredients except olive slices. Spoon egg yolk mixture back into egg white halves. Refrigerate until ready to serve. Garnish with olive slices.

Yield: 12 servings
Calories: 47/serving

A massage will help relax and restore your tense muscles.

DAY 15

Contra-lateral training works your body in a criss-cross manner: one side of your upper body alternated with the other side of your lower body.

CONTRA-LATERAL TRAINING

Nolan Ryan of the Texas Rangers is a great baseball pitcher. During the summer of 1990 he threw the sixth no-hitter of his career, won his 300th major league game, and became the only pitcher to surpass 5,000 career strikeouts.

Throwing a 90-mile-an-hour fast ball is not only hard to hit but it's hard on the pitcher's body. That's why Ryan went on the disabled list several times during the 1990 season. It's not just a coincidence that Nolan Ryan pitched a no-hitter six days after coming off the disabled list. The rest helped him greatly.

Examination of his workout regimen shows classic signs of overtraining. Ryan's customary routine is an assortment of stationary cycling, sprinting backwards and forward, some swimming, throwing a baseball as well as throwing a football, heavy weight work, and light weight work. He does some type of weight training almost every day, even on game days.

As Nolan tried and failed three times to win his 300th game, the press chronicled his every move. After reading about his overtraining problem, I decided to offer my two cents' worth of advice and note it in my weekly fitness column in the *Dallas Times Herald*.

Nolan's extraordinary delivery style puts tremendous overload on the right side of his upper body, since he pitches with his right arm. But it also requires an almost equal overload to be borne by his left leg, since he has to catch and absorb this force with the left side of his lower body.

Trying to solve Nolan's problem forced me to think in the direction of a split routine for one side of his upper body and the opposite side of his lower body; hence, the name *contra-lateral*.

I quickly organized a contra-lateral routine that I thought would work for Ryan and mentioned it in my *Times Herald* article. I never heard back from Nolan, or anyone from the Rangers' club, so I don't know if he ever tried the program. I do know, however, that Ryan soon won his 300th game. And I know that the contra-lateral plan presented here is one of the most effective split routines you'll ever experience.

I've tested it with only five bodybuilders, including Keith and David, but all noted the isolation it produced and the facilitating effect it had on their recovery ability.

On Day 15 and Day 17 you'll work right lower body alternated with left upper body exercises. On Day 16 and Day 18, you'll do the left lower body alternated with the right upper body exercises. You'll rest on Day 19 and 21. In between on Day 20, you'll do a shortened form of both workouts.

Here's the scoop on today's routine.

1. *Right leg curl:* Lie facedown on a standard leg curl machine. Curl only your right leg, using the super-slow protocol. Keep your left leg straight during the entire movement for your right leg. Do not twist your hips in the top position.

2. *Left pulldown on lat machine:* Attach a single handle to the lat machine. Grasp the handle with your left hand and be seated. Pull the handle slowly down to your chest and pause. Your left hand should be supinated in the down position. Return smoothly to the stretched position and repeat.

3. *Right leg extension:* Sit in the leg extension with both feet behind the movement arm. Straighten your right leg slowly in 10 seconds. Keep your left leg relaxed and bent. Lower smoothly and repeat for maximum repetitions.

4. *Left overhead press with dumbbell:* This exercise is best performed seated. Press the dumbbell slowly overhead, but avoid the lockout. Lower smoothly and repeat.

5. *Right leg press:* Keep the repetitions slow and smooth and avoid the tendency to twist. You'll really feel this one in your right thigh.

6. *Left fly with machine:* Although you may use a dumbbell on this movement, you'll feel it better on a pec-dec machine. Place both arms in the starting position, but only use your left. Bring your left arm slowly across your body and contract your left pectoral. Lower smoothly and repeat. Immediately move to the bench press.

7. *Left bench press with machine:* You may use a dumbbell on this exercise, but you'll feel more secure on a machine. Raise and lower the resistance in the super-slow style using only your left arm.

8. *Right calf raise:* Use either a dumbbell or a standing calf-raise machine for this movement. Raise and lower your right heel slowly and smoothly. Keep your knee locked and do not bounce.

9. *Left preacher curl with dumbbell:* Use a high preacher bench with an almost vertical decline. Hang your left arm over the front with a dumbbell in your hand. Curl the dumbbell slowly to the top. Lower smoothly and repeat for maximum repetitions.

10. *Left triceps extension with dumbbell:* Sit with a dumbbell in your left hand. Press it overhead and keep your elbow by your left ear. Lower the dumbbell smoothly and extend it back to the top. Repeat for maximum repetitions.

11. *Back raise:* Do as many slow, smooth repetitions as possible, and immediately do the deadlift. The back raise and the deadlift emphasize both sides of your lower back.

12. *Stiff-legged deadlift:* You'll really feel these in your lower back, especially if you don't quite stand up in the top position.

DAY 15 RECORD

KEITH'S SCHEDULE

6:00am	Wake up!
6:15am	Eat Meal 1.
6:30am	Read newspaper.
7:00am	Get ready for school.
7:30am	Leave for school.
9:00am	Eat Meal 2.
12:00	Eat Meal 3.
3:00pm	Leave school. Return home.
3:30pm	Eat Meal 4.
4:00pm	Relax or take nap.
5:00pm	Leave for gym.
5:30pm	Workout.
6:30pm	Return home.
7:00pm	Eat Meal 5.
7:30pm	Read, study, prepare for next day.
10:00pm	Eat Meal 6.
10:30pm	Bedtime.

YOUR SCHEDULE

KEITH'S CALORIES

MEAL 1: BREAKFAST

2 cups Cream of Wheat (regular)	280
4 teaspoons brown sugar	70
2 slices toast	160
3 teaspoons margarine	105
1½ cups nonfat milk	135
1 cup orange juice	120

MEAL 2: SNACK

1 plain bagel	190
1 ounce cream cheese	100
4 teaspoons jelly/preserves	70
½ cup dried apricots	200

MEAL 3: LUNCH
Cheeseburger:

5 ounces ground beef	300
1½ ounces cheddar cheese	150
1 hamburger bun	200
1 tablespoon mayonnaise	100
1 tomato, sliced	35
3 lettuce leaves	10
20 French fries (2″ long)	300
1½ apples	160

MEAL 4: SNACK

½ 2,200-calorie shake	1,100
1 brownie	100

MEAL 5: DINNER

2 chicken breasts (5.6 ounces, fried)	728
1 cup of beets	60
2 biscuits	200
1½ teaspoons margarine	50
1 cup creamed corn	200
1 cup nonfat milk	90

MEAL 6: SNACK

½ 2,200-calorie shake	1,100
2 brownies	200
Total	**6,513**

YOUR CALORIES

WORKOUT
CONTRA-LATERAL SPLIT:
Right Lower Body, Left Upper Body

EXERCISE	Keith's Wt/Reps	Your Wt/Reps
1 Right leg curl	$\frac{90}{6}$	
2 Left pulldown on lat machine	$\frac{80}{8}$	
3 Right leg extension	$\frac{100}{8}$	
4 Left overhead press with dumbbell	$\frac{55}{7}$	
5 Right leg press	$\frac{205}{10}$	
6 Left fly with machine	$\frac{150}{10}$	
7 Left bench press with machine	$\frac{60}{8}$	
8 Right calf raise	$\frac{80}{6}$	
9 Left preacher curl with dumbbell	$\frac{40}{6}$	
10 Left triceps extension with dumbbell	$\frac{35}{12}$	
11 Back raise	$\frac{Bdwt.+15}{8}$	
12 Stiff-legged deadlift	$\frac{195}{11}$	

89

DAY 16

LEFT LOWER BODY, RIGHT UPPER BODY

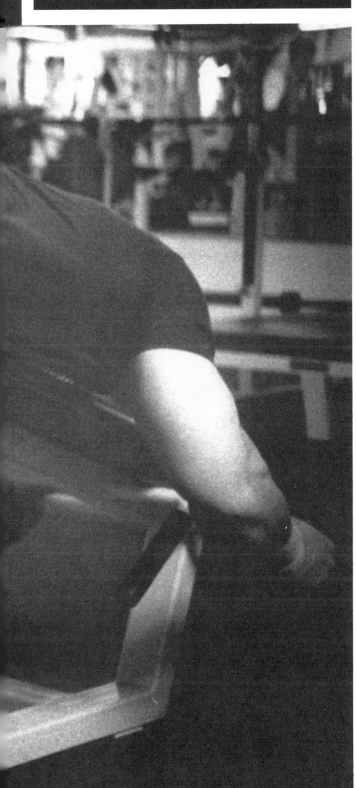

Today, you'll work the left side of your lower body and the right side of your upper body. You'll need to make several modifications toward the end of your workout. Instead of the back raise and the stiff-legged deadlift, substitute the trunk curl and the reverse trunk curl. And lastly, you'll do the 4-way neck machine.

Be sure and keep your eating at an above-adequate level. Study Keith's listings yesterday for suggestions. Write down your food servings in the appropriate spaces and be consistent.

Here are brief notations about your exercise schedule.

1. *Left leg curl:* Do the same thing for your left hamstrings today that you did for your right hamstrings yesterday.

2. *Right pulldown on lat machine:* Stabilize your upper body with your left arm as you do the pulldown with your right arm.

3. *Left leg extension:* Try to keep your face relaxed as you perform the maximum number of super-slow repetitions.

4. *Right overhead press with dumbbell:* A little body sway is permitted in this exercise.

5. *Left leg press:* Your training partner may want to give you a couple of assisted repetitions on this movement.

6. *Right fly with machine:* Try to do at least the same number of repetitions today as you did yesterday. Move quickly to the bench press.

7. *Right bench press with machine:* Avoid locking your arm at the top until your last one or two repetitions.

8. *Left calf raise:* You'll be surprised at how little resistance you can handle on the calf raise, especially if your form is slow and strict. The reason is that you probably failed to account for the fact that you've got your entire body weight on one leg, as opposed to two.

9. *Right preacher curl with dumbbell:* Keep your hips down and you'll be less likely to cheat.

10. *Right triceps extension with dumbbell:* Be smooth at the turnarounds and move slowly.

11. *Trunk curl:* Smoothly curl your torso into the contracted position.

12. *Reverse trunk curl:* Lie on your back with your hands by your hips and flat on the floor. Bend your knees and place your thighs close to your torso and keep them there. This is the starting position. Pull your hips slowly up and toward chest. Your lower back should be off the floor. Pause, lower smoothly, and repeat. You'll feel a strong contraction in your lower abdominals.

13. *4-way neck machine:* Work all four sides of your neck.

On the leg curl concentrate on getting a full range of motion on each repetition.

DAY 16 RECORD

KEITH'S SCHEDULE

6:00am	Wake up!
6:15am	Eat Meal 1.
6:30am	Read newspaper.
7:00am	Get ready for school.
7:30am	Leave for school.
9:00am	Eat Meal 2.
12:00	Eat Meal 3.
3:00pm	Leave school. Return home.
3:30pm	Eat Meal 4.
4:00pm	Relax or take nap.
5:00pm	Leave for gym.
5:30pm	Workout.
6:30pm	Return home.
7:00pm	Eat Meal 5.
7:30pm	Read, study, prepare for next day.
10:00pm	Eat Meal 6.
10:30pm	Bedtime.

YOUR SCHEDULE

YOUR CALORIES

WORKOUT
CONTRA-LATERAL SPLIT:
Left Lower Body, Right Upper Body

EXERCISE	Keith's Wt/Reps	Your Wt/Reps
1 Left leg curl	$\frac{90}{8}$	
2 Right pulldown on lat machine	$\frac{85}{9}$	
3 Left leg extension	$\frac{105}{10}$	
4 Right overhead press	$\frac{55}{10}$	
5 Left leg press	$\frac{205}{10}$	
6 Right fly with machine	$\frac{160}{10}$	
7 Right bench press with machine	$\frac{65}{10}$	
8 Left calf raise	$\frac{60}{9}$	
9 Right preacher curl with dumbbell	$\frac{40}{8}$	
10 Right tricep extension with dumbbell	$\frac{40}{12}$	
11 Trunk curl	$\frac{Bdwt.+25}{10}$	
12 Reverse trunk curl	$\frac{Bdwt.}{6}$	
13 4-way neck machine	$\frac{42.5}{6}$	

In the top position of the calf raise, try to push a little higher by pressing down with your big toe.

DOMINANT ARM SMALLER

An experienced observer at any major body-building championship will notice an interesting comparison among the contestants. In almost all cases the left arm of a right-handed bodybuilder is larger than his right arm, usually to a significant degree.

This is true because the left arm of a right-handed person must work harder to perform its share of an equally divided work load. The left arm does not work more, nor differently—it works harder, with greater intensity of effort. And it responds by growing larger than the right arm.

A right-handed individual lacks some degree of coordination in his left arm. His balance and muscular control are both less efficient in his left arm. This remains true to some degree regardless of the length of time that he has been training both arms identically. Therefore, the left arm works harder, and its response to this increased intensity of effort is to grow. Research shows that in tests of strength that do not involve balance or muscular coordination, the left arm is almost always stronger as well as larger.

When this interesting fact is brought to the attention of most bodybuilders, their response usually is: "Well, in that case, I'll do an extra set of curls and extensions with my right arm. Then it will grow larger, too."

To achieve growth, most bodybuilders assume that more exercise is required when only *harder* exercise is needed.

Lacking the proper intensity of effort, scant results will be produced by any amount of exercise, and certainly none in the areas of muscular size and strength. Given the proper intensity, however, a small amount of exercise will give the best possible results.

Although this has been pointed out repeatedly to bodybuilders, it remains largely misunderstood. The usual practice is to do more individual exercises and more sets of each exercise in the mistaken belief that this increase in amount of exercise will also produce an increase in intensity of effort.

If you have one arm or one leg bigger than the other, you have a chance to correct the situation with the contra-lateral program. Slow, hard, brief exercise is the best way to bring a lagging body part up to par.

Concentrate on your spot-specific weaknesses during the contra-lateral phase and you'll be rewarded with more size, strength, and symmetry.

Your smaller arm needs harder exercise to grow, not more sets or more exercise.

DAY 17

DAY 17 RECORD

KEITH'S SCHEDULE

6:00am	Wake up!
6:15am	Eat Meal 1.
6:30am	Read newspaper.
7:00am	Get ready for school.
7:30am	Leave for school.
9:00am	Eat Meal 2.
12:00	Eat Meal 3.
3:00pm	Leave school.
	Return home.
3:30pm	Eat Meal 4.
4:00pm	Relax or take nap.
5:00pm	Leave for gym.
5:30pm	Workout.
6:30pm	Return home.
7:00pm	Eat Meal 5.
7:30pm	Read, study, prepare for next day.
10:00pm	Eat Meal 6.
10:30pm	Bedtime.

YOUR SCHEDULE

YOUR CALORIES

WORKOUT
CONTRA-LATERAL SPLIT:
Right Lower Body, Left Upper Body

EXERCISE	Keith's Wt/Reps	Your Wt/Reps
1 Right leg curl	$\frac{90}{9}$	
2 Left pulldown on lat machine	$\frac{85}{10}$	
3 Right leg extension	$\frac{105}{10}$	
4 Left overhead press with dumbbell	$\frac{55}{15}$	
5 Right leg press	$\frac{215}{8}$	
6 Left fly with machine	$\frac{170}{10}$	
7 Left bench press with machine	$\frac{70}{10}$	
8 Right calf raise	$\frac{80}{8}$	
9 Left preacher curl with dumbbell	$\frac{45}{8}$	
10 Left triceps extension with dumbbell	$\frac{40}{10}$	
11 Back raise	$\frac{Bdwt.+15}{10}$	
12 Stiff-legged deadlift	$\frac{215}{10}$	

On the triceps extension, keep your upper arm stable and in a vertical position.

DAY 18

PROTEIN FACTS

The facts about protein and muscle building are not at all what the muscle magazines want bodybuilders to believe. Most of them report that "muscles are made up of protein" and "to build large muscles, you need massive amounts of protein."

The physiological fact is that muscles are composed mostly of water. Rarely is an American athlete deficient in protein. In fact, research notes just the opposite. It also shows that athletes, especially bodybuilders and weightlifters, consume three times as much protein per day as they need for maximum muscular growth.

How much protein per day do you need? Here is a guideline: Multiply body weight in pounds by .36 grams. If you weigh 180 pounds, you will require only 64.8 grams daily. Even a 300-pound bodybuilder would need no more than 108 grams daily. Yet the consumption of more than 300 grams of protein per day has become an important necessity for most bodybuilders. Such unscientific eating practices are unnecessary as well as potentially dangerous.

Consuming massive amounts of protein is primarily threatening to the liver and kidneys. These are important organs in the protein utilization process. Since protein cannot be stored to any extent in the body, the metabolism and excretion of nonstorable protein loads can impose serious stress and may cause a dangerous enlargement of two very important organs.

The eating plan recommended in this course contains more than adequate amounts of protein, without being excessive.

Get it out of your mind that you need massive amounts of protein in your system to build larger, stronger muscles. You do *not*.

The dairy products recommended daily in this book provide optimum amounts of protein for maximum muscle building.

DAY 18 RECORD

KEITH'S SCHEDULE

6:00am	Wake up!
6:15am	Eat Meal 1.
6:30am	Read newspaper.
7:00am	Get ready for school.
7:30am	Leave for school.
9:00am	Eat Meal 2.
12:00	Eat Meal 3.
3:00pm	Leave school.
	Return home.
3:30pm	Eat Meal 4.
4:00pm	Relax or take nap.
5:00pm	Leave for gym.
5:30pm	Workout.
6:30pm	Return home.
7:00pm	Eat Meal 5.
7:30pm	Read, study, prepare for next day.
10:00pm	Eat Meal 6.
10:30pm	Bedtime.

YOUR SCHEDULE

YOUR CALORIES

WORKOUT
CONTRA-LATERAL SPLIT:
Left Lower Body, Right Upper Body

EXERCISE	Keith's Wt/Reps	Your Wt/Reps
1 Left leg curl	$\frac{95}{8}$	
2 Right pulldown on lat machine	$\frac{90}{8}$	
3 Left leg extension	$\frac{110}{10}$	
4 Right overhead press	$\frac{60}{10}$	
5 Left leg press	$\frac{225}{7}$	
6 Right fly with machine	$\frac{170}{10}$	
7 Right bench press with machine	$\frac{75}{8}$	
8 Left calf raise	$\frac{80}{8}$	
9 Right preacher curl with dumbbell	$\frac{45}{8}$	
10 Right triceps extension with dumbbell	$\frac{45}{7}$	
11 Trunk curl	$\frac{Bdwt.+35}{9}$	
12 Reverse trunk curl	$\frac{Bdwt.}{8}$	
13 4-way neck machine	$\frac{42.5}{8}$	

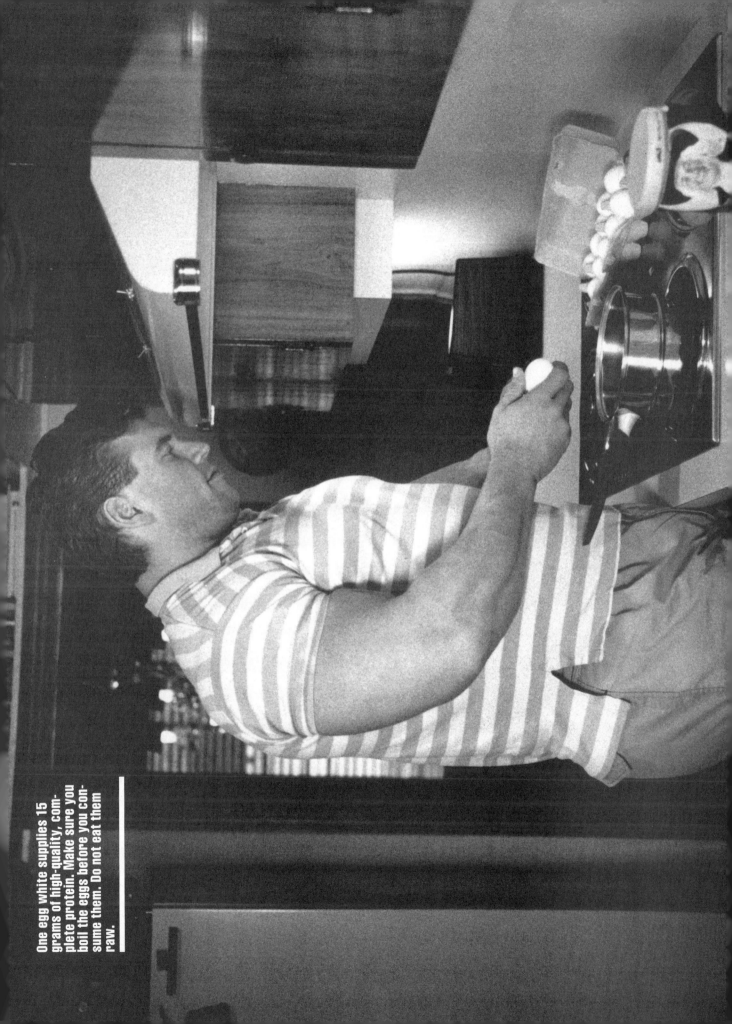

One egg white supplies 15 grams of high-quality, complete protein. Make sure you boil the eggs before you consume them. Do not eat them raw.

The bent-armed fly with dumbbells stretches your pectorals to a maximum degree.

MUSCLES AND SURVIVAL

There is a physiology lesson to be learned from laboratory rats. The work was done by Dr. Alfred L. Goldberg and colleagues and was reported in *Medicine and Science in Sports* (7:248–261, 1975).

Through proper exercise, momentary muscular failure is a stimulation signal for the body to over-compensate. Dr. Goldberg and his researchers at-

tempted to effect just such an overcompensation by reducing the mechanical efficiency of muscle. They did this by surgically cutting the gastrocnemius muscle of one leg of each of a group of rats. Ankle extension was then borne by only the plantaris and soleus muscles.

The rats were then run on a treadmill and the plantaris and soleus of the treated legs grew dramatically compared to their other legs.

Eventually, many research groups of rats underwent unilateral cutting of the gastrocnemius, but some groups received simultaneous and other handicaps. One group was hypophysectomized—the hypophysis of their pituitary removed—so that they could not produce growth hormone. Another group received alloxan, which produces a diabetic state—a lack of insulin. Another group was placed on a starvation diet of only water. Other groups have various combinations of the same procedures.

Once preparation was complete, all the animals were run on treadmills. After an appropriate time they were sacrificed for analysis. The analysis revealed that the plantaris and soleus muscles overcompensated. They grew, apparently at the expense of other body tissues. They grew on a starvation diet, without insulin, and without growth hormone. They grew in spite of the fact that their growth and consumption of resources meant a loss of health.

In plain talk, even though their weight and total muscle mass fell some 30 percent, both their plantaris and soleus muscles actually *increased* in size and weight.

The researchers stumbled into a fundamental biological priority. If stimulated, muscle will grow in spite of tremendous adversity and at the expense of the remainder of the organism.

One of the fundamental traits of animal life is locomotion. Locomotion depends on muscular strength. Survival resources, therefore, are allocated to the muscles first. This priority allocation, however, is predicated upon muscular growth stimulation. Without the stimulation, resources are stored, sloughed off, or put to other uses.

What can you learn from the research with the laboratory rats?

If you are displeased with the size of your muscles, you are not stimulating them to grow. And growth stimulation is a result of *exercise*: pure and simple, *hard, brief, infrequent exercise*.

DAY 19 RECORD

KEITH'S SCHEDULE

6:00am	Wake up!
6:15am	Eat Meal 1.
6:30am	Read newspaper.
7:00am	Get ready for school.
7:30am	Leave for school.
9:00am	Eat Meal 2.
12:00	Eat Meal 3.
3:00pm	Leave school.
	Return home.
3:30pm	Eat Meal 4.
4:00pm	Take a nap.
5:30pm	Freshen up.
5:45pm	Watch TV.
6:30pm	Eat Meal 5.
7:00pm	Attend sporting event.
10:00pm	Return home.
10:30pm	Eat Meal 6.
11:00pm	Bedtime.

YOUR SCHEDULE

YOUR CALORIES

CAJUN-STYLE CHICKEN BREASTS

- ¼ cup butter
- 1 tablespoon freshly squeezed lemon juice
- ¼ teaspoon dried thyme, crushed
- ¼ teaspoon dried oregano, crushed
- ¼ teaspoon cayenne pepper
- ¼ teaspoon finely ground fresh black pepper
  Salt to taste
- 4 boneless skinned chicken breasts (4 ounces each), pounded thin

Melt butter in a small saucepan over a low heat. Add lemon juice, herbs, black pepper, and salt to taste. Continue to cook for several minutes over a low heat until herbs soften.

Heat over a large cast-iron skillet to high. Coat both sides of the breasts well with the butter mixture. Cook the breasts for several minutes on each side. When done, they will be black on the outside and tender and juicy on the inside.

Yield: 4 servings
Calories: 222/serving

WHEAT GERM CHICKEN

- 1 frying or roasting chicken (3½ to 4 pounds), cut up and skinned
- 2 tablespoons safflower oil mixed with 2 tablespoons water
- ½ cup wheat germ
- ½ cup whole wheat flour
- ½ teaspoon poultry seasoning
  Salt and freshly ground pepper to taste

Brush chicken pieces with oil and water mixture. Set them on a rack for several minutes to drain. In a plastic bag, shake wheat germ, flour, and seasonings to mix. Then shake each piece of chicken in the plastic bag until coated with the wheat germ mixture. Place them evenly apart on a baking rack, and bake them in a 375° oven for 45–50 minutes.

Yield: 4 servings
Calories: 385/serving

Triceps extensions may be performed with a barbell, a dumbbell, or a machine.

20

CONTRA-LATERAL COMBINATION

By now you should be getting accustomed to the contra-lateral training. It's different, isn't it? But *it's* also very productive.

"It's weird having only one side of your upper body and the other side of your lower body sore," Keith Whitley said after his first contra-lateral workout. "But I guess it balances out after a week."

It does balance out. In fact, today's training session is a combination workout. You'll do a simplified version of the workout you did on Day 15 combined with Day 16. You'll also work your arms together.

Here is the order.

1. *Right leg curl*
2. *Left pulldown on lat machine*
3. *Right leg extension*
4. *Left overhead press with dumbbell*
5. *Left fly with machine*
6. *Left bench press with machine*
7. *Left leg curl*
8. *Right pulldown on lat machine*
9. *Left leg extension*
10. *Right overhead press with dumbbell*
11. *Right fly with machine*
12. *Right bench press with machine*
13. *One-repetition chin-up:* Try to make this exercise as intense and slow as possible by taking from 30–60 seconds to pull up and another 30–60 seconds to lower. Use an underhanded, shoulder-width grip on the overhead bar. Rush to the next exercise.
14. *Biceps curl with barbell:* After the chin-up you won't be able to handle much weight on the curl, perhaps 50 percent of what you normally use. Take an underhanded grip on the barbell and stand. Anchor your elbows against the sides of your waist and keep them there throughout the movement. Lean forward slightly. Look down at your hands and curl the weight slowly in 10 seconds. Lower the bar smoothly and repeat for maximum repetitions.
15. *One-repetition dip:* Perform the dip in a similar manner as the one-repetition chin-up. Take 30 to 60 seconds to move to the top and an equal amount of time to lower. Rush to the triceps extension.
16. *Triceps extension with one dumbbell held in both hands:* Hold a dumbbell at one end with both hands and press it overhead. Do as many super-slow repetitions as possible. Don't quit until you've tried, for at least 10 seconds, to move the dumbbell past the sticking point on the last repetition.

Today, you'll work your right leg, and a bit later, you'll exercise your left leg.

DAY 20 RECORD

KEITH'S SCHEDULE

7:00am	Wake up!
7:15am	Eat Meal 1.
7:30am	Read newspaper.
8:00am	Do home chores.
10:00am	Eat Meal 2.
10:30am	Wash cars.
12:00	Eat Meal 3.
12:30pm	Go grocery shopping.
3:00pm	Return home.
3:15pm	Eat Meal 4.
5:00pm	Leave for workout.
5:30pm	Workout.
6:30pm	Return home.
7:00pm	Eat Meal 5.
7:30pm	Go to movie.
11:00pm	Return home.
11:15pm	Eat Meal 6.
11:30pm	Bedtime.

YOUR SCHEDULE

YOUR CALORIES

WORKOUT
CONTRA-LATERAL SPLIT:
Combination

EXERCISE	Keith's Wt/Reps	Your Wt/Reps
1 Right leg curl	$\frac{100}{9}$	
2 Left pulldown on lat machine	$\frac{95}{8}$	
3 Right leg extension	$\frac{115}{10}$	
4 Left overhead press with dumbbell	$\frac{65}{10}$	
5 Left fly with machine	$\frac{180}{10}$	
6 Left bench press with machine	$\frac{80}{9}$	
7 Left leg curl	$\frac{100}{9}$	
8 Right pulldown on lat machine	$\frac{95}{7}$	
9 Left leg extension	$\frac{115}{10}$	
10 Right overhead press with dumbbell	$\frac{65}{10}$	
11 Right fly with machine	$\frac{180}{10}$	
12 Right bench press with machine	$\frac{80}{8}$	
13 One-repetition chin-up	$\frac{25'P}{20'N}$	
14 Biceps curl with barbell	$\frac{85}{9}$	
15 One-repetition dip	$\frac{30'P}{30'N}$	
16 Triceps extension with one dumbbell held in both hands	$\frac{70}{8}$	

On the one-armed pulldown, it may be helpful to anchor your off-shoulder by holding the frame of the lat machine.

DAY 21

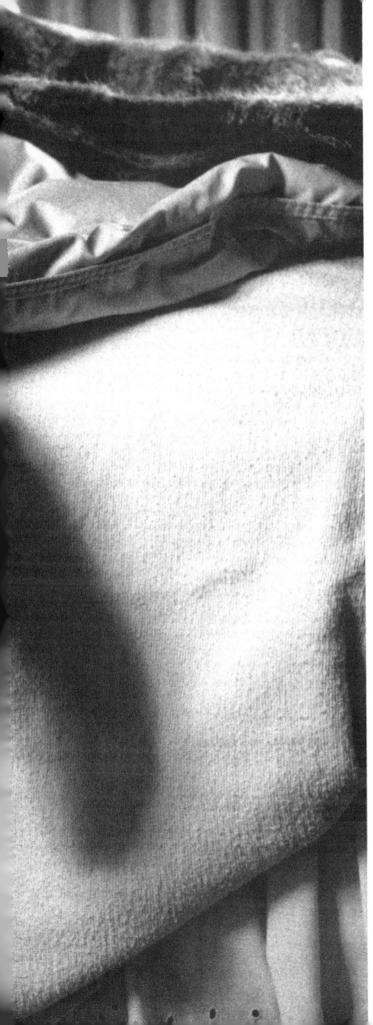

SLEEP GUIDELINES

The actual growth process involved in building muscle does not occur during exercising or eating. It occurs during resting situations, primarily while you are asleep.

It is essential, therefore, that you get at least 8 hours of sleep each night. Teenagers on the program, in fact, will be better off trying to get approximately 10 hours nightly.

Newborn babies, who have phenomenal growth rates, sleep an average of 16 to 18 hours a day. By age 1, they are down to 13 to 14 hours of daily sleep.

As youngsters get older, their need for sleep gradually decreases until it levels off in adolescence. Teenagers generally require 9½ hours of rest a day.

Sleep time tapers off once again in adulthood. Most people find they need about 8 hours. Approximately 10 percent require significantly more or less sleep.

Contrary to common belief, the need for sleep does not decline in later years. Instead, the elderly find that their sleep becomes more restless.

Both Keith and David tried to get as much sleep as they could during the 42-day program. Any time they could catch an extra hour, especially on weekends, they did so. An occasional 15-to-30-minute midafternoon nap was also refreshing.

Both Keith and David commented that the 42-day eating and exercising plan helped them to sleep more soundly. This reinforces the fact that research finds that sound sleep is more effective than restless sleep. You certainly sleep better when you're tired, and as you are well aware, this course is guaranteed to make you tired.

Here are a few additional tips to help you sleep more soundly:

- Make sure your bedroom is dark, quiet, and comfortably cool.
- Arrange your alarm clock so you can't hear it ticking in the middle of the night.
- Wake up at the same time every morning. If you feel you need more sleep, go to bed earlier, rather than sleeping later.
- Don't eat or drink anything with caffeine in it after lunch.
- Avoid alcohol in the evening. Although it is initially calming, it interferes with the soundness of the sleep.

Teenagers on the Bigger program should strive to get 10 hours of sleep each night.

111

DAY 21 RECORD

KEITH'S SCHEDULE

8:00am	Wake up!
8:15am	Eat Meal 1.
8:30am	Read newspaper.
10:00am	Eat Meal 2.
10:30am	Attend church.
12:30pm	Eat buffet brunch, Meals 3 & 4.
1:30pm	Return home.
2:00pm	Watch TV.
4:00pm	Take a nap.
5:30pm	Enjoy drive or walk.
7:00pm	Eat Meal 5.
7:30pm	Relax or prepare for next day.
10:00pm	Eat Meal 6.
10:30pm	Bedtime.

YOUR SCHEDULE

YOUR CALORIES

SHRIMP AND BROCCOLI

- 1 tablespoon butter
- 2 tablespoons onion, finely minced
- 1 cup nonfat milk
- 2 tablespoons whole wheat pastry flour
- 4 ounces aged cheddar cheese, grated
- ⅛ teaspoon freshly ground white pepper
- 3 cups broccoli florets, steamed
- 1 pound fresh medium-size shrimp, peeled and deveined Juice of ½ lemon
- 2 tablespoons toasted wheat germ Paprika to taste

Melt butter in a small saucepan over a low heat. Quickly sauté onions, then add ⅔ cup of the milk and stir until hot. Blend remaining ⅓ cup of milk with flour and add to saucepan. Stir over a medium heat until mixture thickens. Add cheese and pepper and continue to stir until cheese melts.

Arrange broccoli and shrimp in a 9 × 12-inch baking dish. Squeeze lemon juice over the top, then cover with cheese sauce. Sprinkle with wheat germ and paprika and bake in a 350° oven for 20–25 minutes.

Yield: 6 servings
Calories: 201/serving

BROWNIES

- 2 ounces unsweetened chocolate
- ½ cup margarine
- 1 cup sugar
- 2 eggs
- 1 teaspoon vanilla
- ⅔ cup all-purpose flour
- ½ teaspoon baking powder
- ½ cup chopped pecans

Heat oven on 350°F. Spray 8 × 8 × 2-inch baking pan with vegetable spray. Melt chocolate and margarine in saucepan over low heat. Remove from heat. Add sugar, eggs, and vanilla and beat until smooth. Stir in remaining ingredients and spread in pan. Bake 25 minutes or until brownies start to pull away from sides of pan. Cool slightly. Cut into 1½ × 1½-inch squares.

Yield: 20 brownies
Calories: 128/brownie

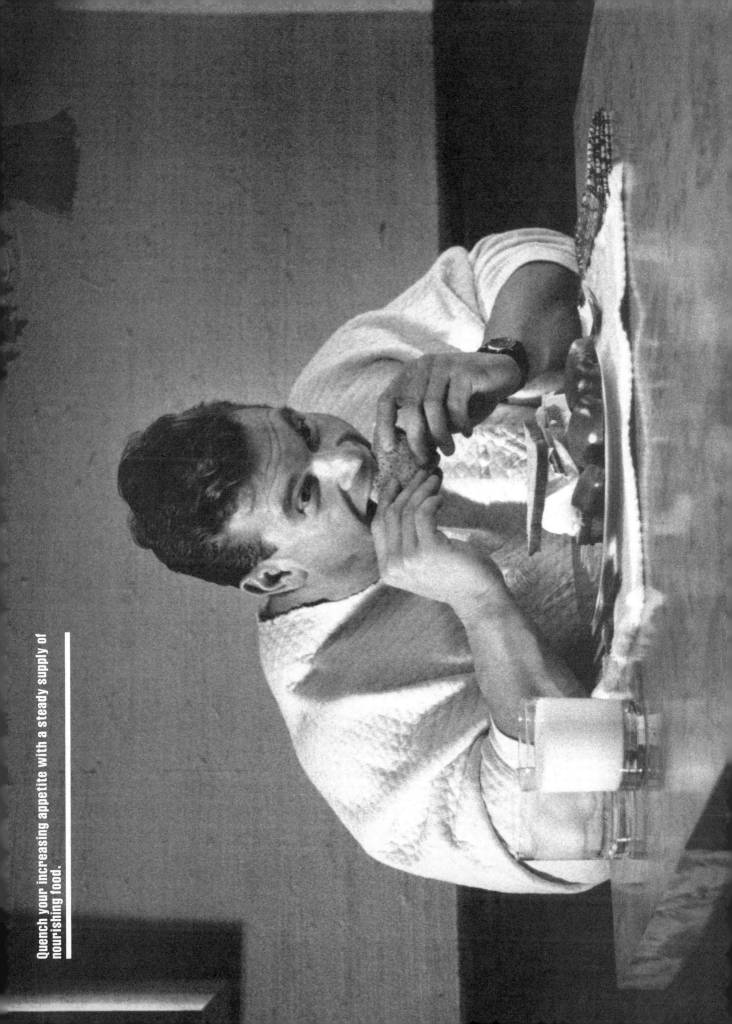

Quench your increasing appetite with a steady supply of nourishing food.

PROGRESS CHECK

This is the halfway point in the 42-day plan to get bigger. How are you doing? Are you bigger, significantly bigger?

Both Keith and David at this stage had already added over 15 pounds of mass to each of their bodies. But was it all muscle?

No, not entirely. I took their skinfold measurements again at the same sites and concluded that each had only a slight increase in body fat. It was not enough to indicate a change in their eating schedules.

We all agreed that so far the program was working well. And we all committed to follow through with even more enthusiasm for the next 21 days.

I hope you are also enthused about your results so far. If, however, you are dissatisfied with your progress, please ask yourself these questions:

- Are you following the routines exactly as directed: If not, you may be neglecting an important exercise.
- Are you being pushed to momentary muscular failure on all your exercises? If not, then your muscles are not being stimulated to grow in the most efficient manner.
- Are you performing each repetition in the recommended super-slow style? Super-slow is harder to learn and more difficult to apply than other faster styles. But it is also more productive.
- Are you getting sufficient rest and relaxation between your workouts? For building maximum muscle mass, it's a good idea to keep other fitness activities to a minimum. And don't forget, 8 hours or more sleep a night is essential.
- Are you eating the recommended servings and calories each day? If not, you may be getting an inadequate ratio of carbohydrates, fats, and proteins. And your calories may not be at a high enough level.

To guarantee their continued mass building, Keith's daily calorie consumption was bumped to 7,000 and David's was increased to 4,600. Be sure and add to your level accordingly.

Your contra-lateral workout schedule for this week will remain similar to last week, with the change occurring in the frequency. The frequency of the workouts will decrease from five per week to four per week. The combination workout will be omitted this week and a rest day will be added on Wednesday, Day 24.

It's okay to perform a few minutes of stationary cycling as a heart-lung warm-up prior to your super-slow workout.

DAY 22

DAY 22 RECORD

KEITH'S SCHEDULE

6:00am	Wake up!
6:15am	Eat Meal 1.
6:30am	Read newspaper.
7:00am	Get ready for school.
7:30am	Leave for school.
9:00am	Eat Meal 2.
12:00	Eat Meal 3.
3:00pm	Leave school. Return home.
3:30pm	Eat Meal 4.
4:00pm	Relax or take nap.
5:00pm	Leave for gym.
5:30pm	Workout.
6:30pm	Return home.
7:00pm	Eat Meal 5.
7:30pm	Read, study, prepare for next day.
10:00pm	Eat Meal 6.
10:30pm	Bedtime.

YOUR SCHEDULE

_____ _____
_____ _____
_____ _____
_____ _____
_____ _____
_____ _____
_____ _____
_____ _____
_____ _____
_____ _____
_____ _____
_____ _____
_____ _____
_____ _____
_____ _____
_____ _____
_____ _____
_____ _____
_____ _____
_____ _____
_____ _____
_____ _____

KEITH'S CALORIES

MEAL 1: BREAKFAST

6 pancakes (4" dia., from mix)	360
8 teaspoons syrup	140
2 teaspoons butter	70
½ cup prunes with pits	280
1 cup nonfat milk	90
½ cup grapefruit juice	60

MEAL 2: SNACK

2 bran muffins (from mix)	280
2 teaspoons butter/margarine	70
1 cup orange sections (fresh or canned)	130
1 apple	80
1 cup nonfat milk	90

MEAL 3: LUNCH

5 ounces baked ham	400
4 slices bread	320
2 tablespoons peanut butter	190
2 tablespoons preserves	100
1 small plum	15
1 cup tomato juice	50
½ cantaloupe	50

MEAL 4: SNACK

½ 2,400-calorie shake	1,200
4 chocolate chip cookies	200

MEAL 5: DINNER

7½ ounces lean steak, broiled	500
1 cup mushrooms	20
2 cups blackeyed peas	380
1 baked potato with skin	220
1 cup canned carrots	34
3 slices French bread	300

MEAL 6: SNACK

½ 2,400-calorie shake	1,200
4 chocolate chip cookies	200
Total	**7,029**

YOUR CALORIES

_____
_____
_____
_____
_____
_____
_____
_____
_____
_____
_____
_____
_____
_____
_____
_____
_____

WORKOUT
CONTRA-LATERAL SPLIT:
Right Lower Body, Left Upper Body

EXERCISE	Keith's Wt/Reps	Your Wt/Reps
1 Right leg curl	105/7	
2 Left pulldown on lat machine	100/8	
3 Right leg extension	120/9	
4 Left overhead press with dumbbell	65/9	
5 Right leg press	215/10	
6 Left fly with machine	190/9	
7 Left bench press with machine	85/7	
8 Right calf raise	80/9	
9 Left preacher curl with dumbbell	50/7	
10 Left triceps extension with dumbbell	45/10	
11 Back raise	Bdwt.+20/8	
12 Stiff-legged deadlift	225/8	

_____ _____
_____ _____
_____ _____
_____ _____
_____ _____
_____ _____
_____ _____
_____ _____
_____ _____
_____ _____
_____ _____
_____ _____
_____ _____
_____ _____
_____ _____

Your body weight should be
steadily increasing.

PARALLEL-GRIP PULLDOWNS

The latissimus dorsi are the largest, strongest muscles of the upper body. When highly developed, they add impressive width and thickness not only to your upper back, but also to your chest.

Many bodybuilders, however, fail to get complete development of these muscles primarily because they are victims of a prevailing misconception. This misconception involves the hand spacing and grip.

Most bodybuilders perform exercises for the latissimus dorsi muscles with a wide grip. The wide-hand spacing, they say, provides more stretch and a greater range of movement for these muscles. A wide grip, in fact, provides less stretch for the latissimus muscles than would afforded by a narrow grip. Furthermore, the wide grip actually prevents a greater range of movement by allowing the upper arms less rotation around the shoulders.

All forms of chinning and pulldown exercises for the latissimus dorsi muscles involve working the biceps of the upper arms. The biceps are smaller and weaker than the latissimus muscles, and this weakness prevents you from working the upper back as hard as is possible. This being true, why do most bodybuilders work their latissimus muscles with the arms in their weakest possible position?

The biceps are strongest for bending when the hands are in a supinated position. Yet most bodybuilders work their latissimus dorsi muscles with their arms in the opposite position. Turning the hands until they are fully supinated (palms up) significantly increases the bending strength of the arms. It is then possible to work the latissimus muscles harder than would be possible with the hands pronated (palms down).

When the elbows are held back in line with the shoulders, as is done in behind-neck chinning and pulldown exercises, the fully supinated position of the hands requires a parallel grip (palms facing one another). Parallel grip bars are now available in most gyms or can be purchased from various mail-order equipment companies.

An understanding of the specific actions of your major muscles is a vital step toward efficient bodybuilding. Do not fall into the trap of doing an exercise because you like it or avoiding an exercise because it is difficult. In general, the harder an exercise, the better the results. As an efficient bodybuilder, you should *not* look for ways to make exercises easier. Look for ways to make them harder and thus more productive.

The pulldown behind neck is best done with a parallel grip bar.

DAY 23

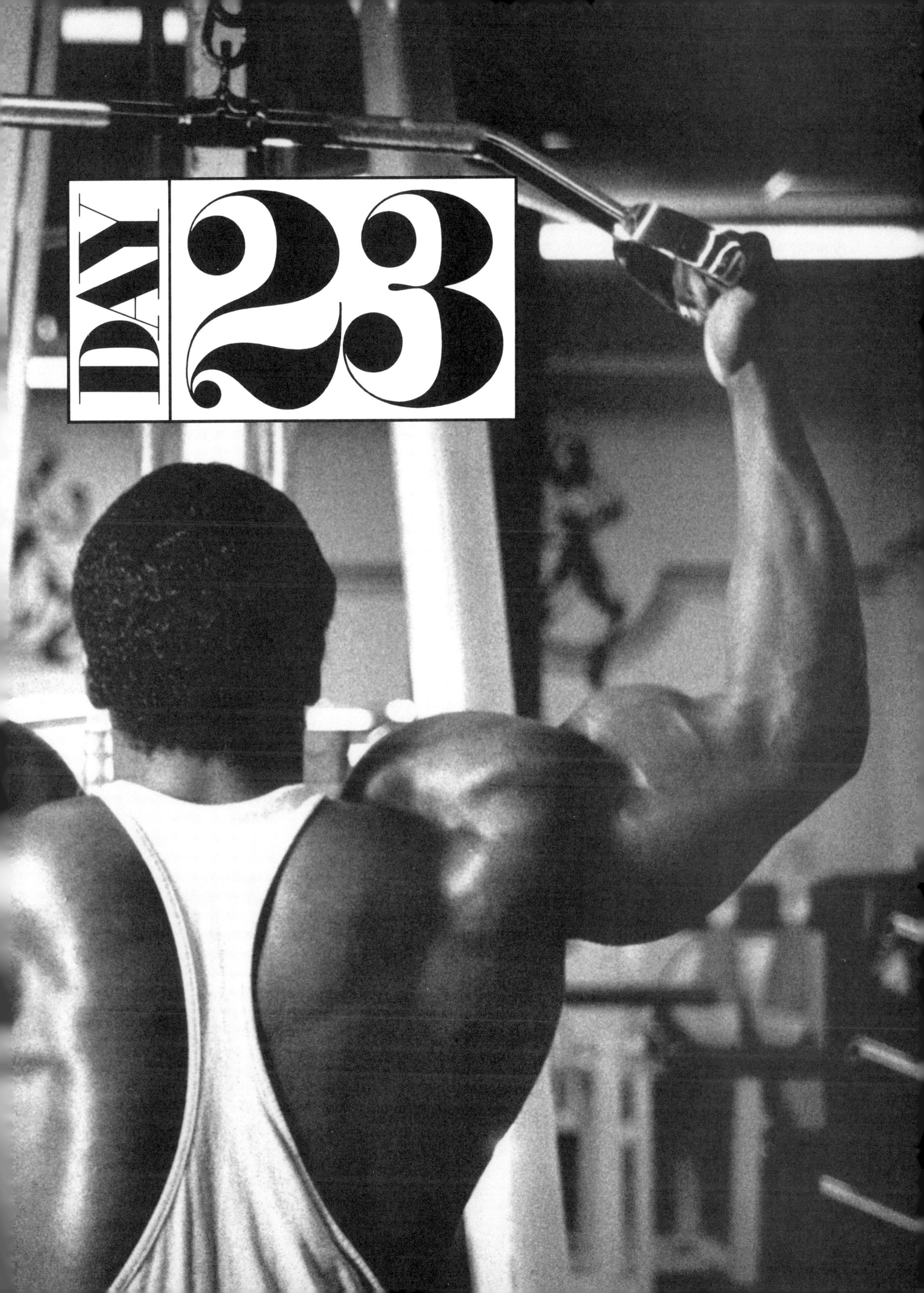

DAY 23 RECORD

KEITH'S SCHEDULE

6:00am	Wake up!
6:15am	Eat Meal 1.
6:30am	Read newspaper.
7:00am	Get ready for school.
7:30am	Leave for school.
9:00am	Eat Meal 2.
12:00	Eat Meal 3.
3:00pm	Leave school.
	Return home.
3:30pm	Eat Meal 4.
4:00pm	Relax or take nap.
5:00pm	Leave for gym.
5:30pm	Workout.
6:30pm	Return home.
7:00pm	Eat Meal 5.
7:30pm	Read, study, prepare for next day.
10:00pm	Eat Meal 6.
10:30pm	Bedtime.

YOUR SCHEDULE

YOUR CALORIES

WORKOUT
CONTRA-LATERAL SPLIT:
Left Lower Body, Right Upper Body

EXERCISE	Keith's Wt/Reps	Your Wt/Reps
1 Left leg curl	$\frac{105}{7}$	
2 Right pulldown on lat machine	$\frac{100}{9}$	
3 Left leg extension	$\frac{125}{10}$	
4 Right overhead press	$\frac{70}{10}$	
5 Left leg press	$\frac{225}{11}$	
6 Right fly with machine	$\frac{200}{10}$	
7 Right bench press with machine	$\frac{80}{11}$	
8 Left calf raise	$\frac{85}{8}$	
9 Right preacher curl with dumbbell	$\frac{50}{8}$	
10 Right triceps extension with dumbbell	$\frac{50}{9}$	
11 Trunk curl	$\frac{Bdwt.+45}{8}$	
12 Reverse trunk curl	$\frac{Bdwt.}{9}$	
13 4-way neck machine	$\frac{45}{8}$	

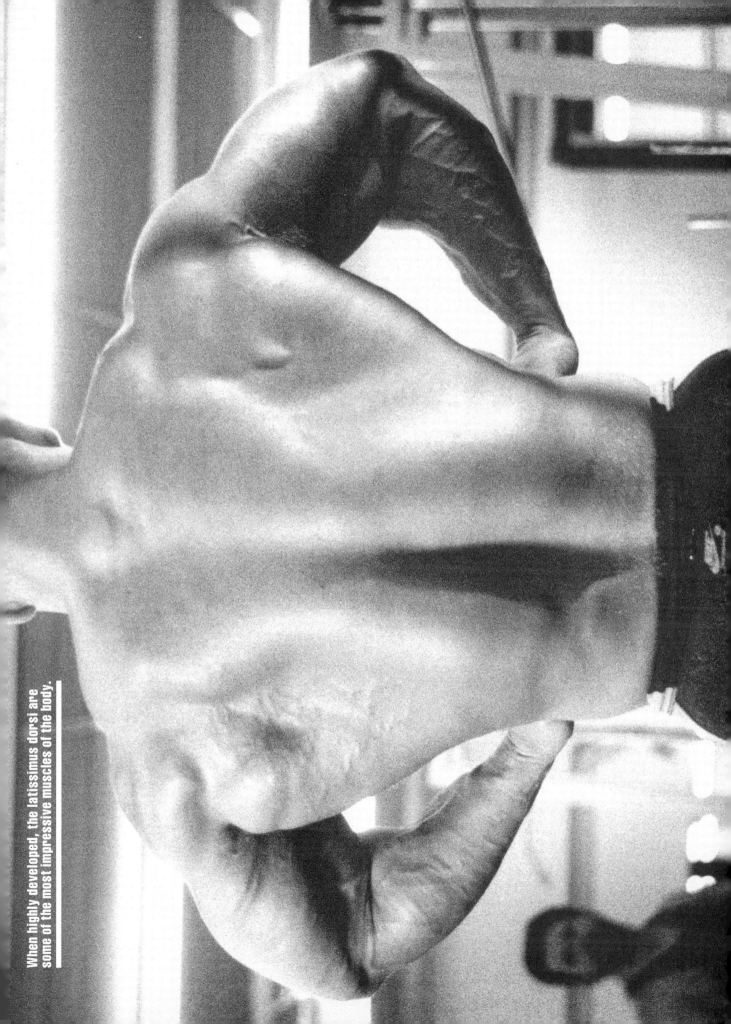

When highly developed, the latissimus dorsi are some of the most impressive muscles of the body.

LONG AND SHORT MUSCLES

Excessively large muscular size is primarily determined by the involved muscle bellies being extremely wide. Wide muscle bellies are the result of having long muscles.

A muscle's length is measured from the tendon attachment at one end to the tendon attached at the other end. The longer a bodybuilder's muscles, the greater the cross-sectional area and the volume of the muscles can become.

A short muscle cannot be very wide because its angle of pull would be so poor that it would not be able to function efficiently. The body, therefore, would not allow a short, wide muscle to develop.

The length of your muscles is 100 percent genetic. You cannot lengthen them through exercise, nutrition, or anything else. What you are born with is what you die with.

All the competitors in the most recent Mr. Olympic contest had long muscles in most of their major body parts. This accounts, in part, for their great size and shape. All champion bodybuilders have great genetics on their side.

Several simple tests to determine biceps and triceps length and potential are described on pages 82–84 of my book *100 High-Intensity Ways to Improve Your Bodybuilding*. Generally, the longer your biceps and triceps are, the larger your upper arms will be, or at least the larger they will be after proper training.

Keith Whitley has long muscles, especially in his calves, thighs, hips, chest, and forearms. This accounts for much of his mass-building potential.

Regardless of the length of your major muscles, the program in this book will help build them to their fullest potential.

Keith Whitley has long pectoral muscles.

DAY 21

DAY 24 RECORD

KEITH'S SCHEDULE

6:00am	Wake up!
6:15am	Eat Meal 1.
6:30am	Read newspaper.
7:00am	Get ready for school.
7:30am	Leave for school.
9:00am	Eat Meal 2.
12:00	Eat Meal 3.
3:00pm	Leave school.
	Return home.
3:30pm	Eat Meal 4.
4:00pm	Take a nap.
5:30pm	Freshen up.
5:45pm	Watch TV.
6:30pm	Eat Meal 5.
7:00pm	Read, study, prepare for next day.
9:30pm	Eat Meal 6.
10:00pm	Bedtime.

YOUR SCHEDULE

YOUR CALORIES

TURKEY VEGETABLE GUMBO

1½ pounds meaty turkey pieces with bones, cooked or uncooked
6 cups water
2 cloves garlic, peeled
2 bay leaves
1 medium onion, chopped
2 large ripe tomatoes, peeled, seeded, and chopped
1 cup fresh or frozen corn
1½ cups fresh or frozen okra, sliced
¼ cup fresh parsley, chopped
1 teaspoon each dried marjoram and thyme
¼ teaspoon red pepper flakes
Salt to taste

Put turkey pieces, water, garlic, and bay leaves in a large kettle or stockpot and bring to a boil. Lower heat, partially cover, and simmer about 1–1½ hours until turkey meat begins to fall from the bones. Strain broth, and reserve turkey pieces. Chill, and skim any fat off the top.

Pour stock back into the pot with remaining ingredients. Simmer covered for 10 minutes. Remove turkey from bones and discard any skin. Cut turkey chunks into bite-size pieces and add to the gumbo. Simmer 5 more minutes.

Yield: 6 servings
Calories: 214/serving

SNACK NOUGATS

½ cup peanut butter
½ cup honey
¾ cup skim milk powder
½ cup toasted wheat germ

Blend peanut butter and honey in small bowl. In a separate small bowl mix milk powder and wheat germ together. Gradually stir dry mixture into peanut butter–honey mixture. Spread on waxed paper and knead until well blended. Pat down until ½-inch thick and cut into 1-inch squares. Chill in refrigerator and store in covered container.

Yield: 12 squares
Calories: 75/square

Notice the length of Keith's
forearm flexor muscles.

DARK EYES AND LEANNESS

If a computer were programmed to analyze the physical characteristics of the winners of major bodybuilding contests over the last 50 years, an unexpected factor would undoubtedly surface. The vast majority of the winners would have dark eyes, dark hair, and dark skin. A high correlation would exist between low body fat, or muscle definition, and dark skin, eyes and hair. There would be a few light-skinned, blue-eyed, blond-haired champions, but they would be the exception rather than the rule.

Both heat and cold are stressful to the human body. A strong relationship seems to exist between body fat and annual mean temperature. The colder the mean temperature, the fatter people become. The warmer the mean temperature, the leaner they are. The relative leanness of warm-dwelling people and the relative fatness of cold-dwelling people can be traced back to a period roughly 18,000 to 25,000 years ago. In the cold regions of the world during that time period, the ability to store surplus fat under the skin with the least possible total food intake may have made the difference between life and death.

Central heating, air conditioning, and mass production of warm clothing all serve to minimize a modern individual's exposure to environmental extremes. Even so, scientists can document the degree to which the contemporary American still is programmed by blueprints laid down by our Ice Age ancestors.

What do these characteristics mean to the bodybuilder? Generally that bodybuilders with dark skin, hair, and eyes—compared to those with light skin, blond hair, and blue eyes—have a genetic advantage where body leanness and extreme muscular definition are concerned.

Take a good look at fatness or leanness of your mother and father. Do the same for your grandparents. Check out the color of their eyes and hair. Now, reevaluate your body's potential for leanness—and be realistic in your assessment.

At a height of 5′ 8″ and a weight of 225 pounds, muscular Darry Thornton of Dallas plans to enter the National Bodybuilding Championships.

DAY 25 RECORD

KEITH'S SCHEDULE

6:00am	Wake up!
6:15am	Eat Meal 1.
6:30am	Read newspaper.
7:00am	Get ready for school.
7:30am	Leave for school.
9:00am	Eat Meal 2.
12:00	Eat Meal 3.
3:00pm	Leave school. Return home.
3:30pm	Eat Meal 4.
4:00pm	Relax or take nap.
5:00pm	Leave for gym.
5:30pm	Workout.
6:30pm	Return home.
7:00pm	Eat Meal 5.
7:30pm	Read, study, prepare for next day.
10:00pm	Eat Meal 6.
10:30pm	Bedtime.

YOUR SCHEDULE

YOUR CALORIES

WORKOUT
CONTRA-LATERAL SPLIT:
Right Lower Body, Left Upper Body

EXERCISE	Keith's Wt/Reps	Your Wt/Reps
1 Right leg curl	$\frac{110}{6}$	
2 Left pulldown on lat machine	$\frac{105}{8}$	
3 Right leg extension	$\frac{130}{10}$	
4 Left overhead press with dumbbell	$\frac{75}{9}$	
5 Right leg press	$\frac{240}{10}$	
6 Left fly with machine	$\frac{210}{10}$	
7 Left bench press with machine	$\frac{90}{7}$	
8 Right calf raise	$\frac{85}{8}$	
9 Left preacher curl with dumbbell	$\frac{50}{9}$	
10 Left triceps extension with dumbbell	$\frac{50}{10}$	
11 Back raise	$\frac{Bdwt.+20}{10}$	
12 Stiff-legged deadlift	$\frac{235}{8}$	

Darry Thornton's ancestors lived in Haiti, one of the warmer regions of the world.

DAY 26

High-calorie milk shakes made it possible for Keith to easily consume up to 8,000 calories a day.

CALORIE-DENSE BLENDER DRINKS

In your quest to get bigger in 42 days, you may want to use a blender to help you consume the required number of calories each day. Suspending small particles of food in a solution and drinking them speeds up the digestion process.

Many high-caloric foods may be combined and blended effectively for a calorie-dense shake. Some of the recommended foods are:

- Nonfat milk
- Sweetened condensed milk
- Ice milk
- Egg whites
- Chocolate syrup
- Bananas
- Peaches
- Honey
- Nonfat milk powder
- Malted milk powder
- Wheat germ oil
- Safflower oil

Keith Whitley consumed a hefty blender drink almost every day of the program. Below are the ingredients, with calorie listings, for three of his favorites.

CHOCOLATE MALT

		Calories
3	cups nonfat milk	270
2	cups ice milk	370
3	egg whites, soft boiled	45
¼	cup safflower oil	481
3	tablespoons chocolate syrup	150
1	tablespoon peanut butter	95
3	tablespoons corn syrup	180
3	tablespoons malted milk powder	176
		1,767

BANANA SHAKE

		Calories
3	cups nonfat milk	270
2	cups ice milk	370
3	egg whites, soft boiled	45
¼	cup safflower oil	481
1	cup nonfat milk powder	245
2	bananas	200
4	tablespoons molasses	200
½	cup cold water	0
		1,811

FRUIT SHAKE

		Calories
3	cups nonfat milk	270
2	cups ice milk	370
3	egg whites, soft boiled	45
¼	cup safflower oil	481
3	peaches without pits	120
5	ozs. frozen strawberries (sweetened)	155
1	banana	100
3	dried apricots	55
2	tablespoons honey	130
		1,726

Generally, the first four ingredients in all of Keith's blender drinks are the same. The other items are usually flavorings and carbohydrate-rich sweeteners.

The egg whites are always lightly cooked, as opposed to raw. Raw eggs can cause food poisoning, and cooked eggs are more nutritious. After soft-boiling the eggs, the yolks are discarded. The yolks are high in cholesterol.

Safflower oil is high in polyunsaturated fatty acids and mixes well with other ingredients. It is relatively inexpensive compared to wheat germ oil and the various medium-chain triglyceride oils, and it is certainly a calorie-dense food.

Each of the three drinks above contains approximately 1,800 calories, and each one has the recommended ratio among carbohydrates, fats, and proteins. To increase the calories per day of each shake, while keeping the same ratio, add the same percentage—10 percent, for example—to each ingredient. That's basically what Keith did each week to increase the calories of his blender drinks.

DAY 26 RECORD

KEITH'S SCHEDULE

6:00am	Wake up!
6:15am	Eat Meal 1.
6:30am	Read newspaper.
7:00am	Get ready for school.
7:30am	Leave for school.
9:00am	Eat Meal 2.
12:00	Eat Meal 3.
3:00pm	Leave school.
	Return home.
3:30pm	Eat Meal 4.
4:00pm	Relax or take nap.
5:00pm	Leave for gym.
5:30pm	Workout.
6:30pm	Return home.
7:00pm	Eat Meal 5.
7:30pm	Attend sporting event
10:00	Return home.
10:30pm	Eat Meal 6.
11:00pm	Bedtime.

YOUR SCHEDULE

YOUR CALORIES

WORKOUT CONTRA-LATERAL SPLIT:
Left Lower Body, Right Upper Body

EXERCISE	Keith's Wt/Reps	Your Wt/Reps
1 Left leg curl	$\frac{110}{7}$	
2 Right pulldown on lat machine	$\frac{110}{8}$	
3 Left leg extension	$\frac{135}{10}$	
4 Right overhead press	$\frac{80}{9}$	
5 Left leg press	$\frac{250}{11}$	
6 Right fly with machine	$\frac{220}{10}$	
7 Right bench press with machine	$\frac{100}{7}$	
8 Left calf raise	$\frac{90}{6}$	
9 Right preacher curl with dumbbell	$\frac{55}{7}$	
10 Right triceps extension with dumbbell	$\frac{55}{5}$	
11 Trunk curl	$\frac{Bdwt.+45}{10}$	
12 Reverse trunk curl	$\frac{Bdwt.}{10}$	
13 4-way neck machine	$\frac{50}{6}$	

DAY 27

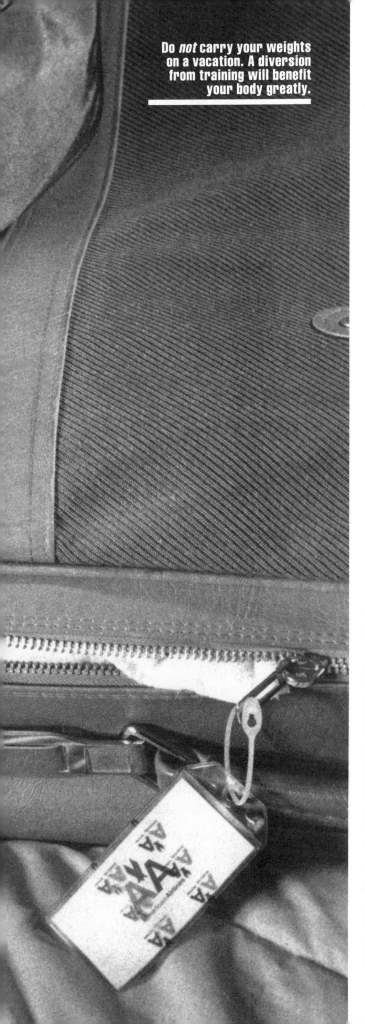

Do *not* carry your weights on a vacation. A diversion from training will benefit your body greatly.

LAYOFFS AND VACATIONS

Day 27 and Day 28 are back-to-back rest days. You'll need the next 48 hours to replenish your recovery ability and ready yourself for the next two weeks of the program.

In the meantime, it's an appropriate time to discuss layoffs and vacations.

Your bodybuilding routine should never be permitted to degenerate into a rut. If you merely go through the motions without extending yourself, boredom is bound to plague you. If you become bored, your training will not produce worthwhile results, and if this continues long enough, you may lose interest in exercise of any kind.

Best bodybuilding results are produced if layoffs are occasionally permitted, as long as they are not scheduled in advance. If you look forward to a scheduled layoff, your incentive is diminished. If you are forced to take an unexpected layoff, you will return to training with new enthusiasm.

Apart from psychological considerations, it is true that the body requires such breaks. A proper layoff should involve at least a week of inactivity. In some cases one solid month away from exercising will do more good than six months of steady training.

If any degree of muscular size or strength is lost, it will be reestablished within a short time. In most cases progress toward unprecedented levels of ability will follow.

In fact, a best performance in many types of sports can only be produced after a layoff. Powerlifters, for example, are well advised to avoid training entirely for three or four days prior to a contest. While a longer layoff might result in a reduced performance, a few days out of training often makes it possible to lift more than ever before. Similar results can be observed in those sport activities that require brief but very intense effort: pole-vaulting, shot-putting, and sprinting are examples.

In almost all cases, if one month of regular training fails to produce marked improvement, the need for a layoff is indicated. Again, the layoff should last at least a full week. Ten days would be better yet, since training could normally be terminated on a Friday and resumed on Monday of the second following week. Two weekends of rest can sometimes do wonders for a bodybuilder's progress.

Individuals differ in their reactions to exercise after a layoff, but in most cases training should be resumed at the same level at which it was terminated.

Except in instances involving injuries or illness, layoffs from training should never exceed one month. Within 30 days, all normal physiological requirements for a break in training will surely have been met.

135

DAY 27 RECORD

KEITH'S SCHEDULE

7:00am	Wake up!
7:15am	Eat Meal 1.
7:30am	Read newspaper.
8:00am	Do home chores.
10:00am	Eat Meal 2.
10:30am	Wash cars.
12:00	Eat Meal 3.
12:30pm	Go grocery shopping.
3:00pm	Return home.
3:15pm	Eat Meal 4.
3:30pm	Take a nap.
5:30pm	Go out to eat Meal 5.
7:30pm	Go to movie.
10:30pm	Return home.
11:00pm	Eat Meal 6.
11:30pm	Bedtime.

YOUR SCHEDULE

YOUR CALORIES

TURKEY/CRANBERRY STIR-FRY

- ⅔ cup freshly squeezed orange juice
- 2 tablespoons low-sodium tamari
- 2 tablespoons rice vinegar
- 12 ounces cooked turkey breast, cut in strips
- 1 tablespoon peanut oil
- 2 ribs celery, diced
- 2 green onions, chopped
- 1 cup whole cranberry relish
- 1 tablespoon grated orange rind
- ¼ cup chopped walnuts

Combine orange juice, tamari, and vinegar in a large bowl. Marinate turkey pieces in the mixture for 1 hour. Heat oil in a wok or large nonstick skillet. Stir-fry celery and green onions until celery is tender-crisp. Add turkey and toss until hot. Stir in cranberry relish, orange rind, and walnuts. Add any remaining marinade and stir quickly over a medium-high heat until most of the liquid has evaporated.

Yield: 4 servings
Calories: 358/serving

CUCUMBER EGG SALAD

- 2 medium cucumbers
- 2 ribs celery, thinly sliced
- 2 green onions, chopped
- 2 tablespoons fresh parsley, snipped (reserve 1 tablespoon)
- 1 tablespoon fresh dill, snipped
- 2 tablespoons safflower oil mayonnaise
- 2 tablespoons buttermilk
- ⅛ teaspoon freshly ground pepper
  Salt to taste
- 6 hard-boiled eggs, cut into bite-sized chunks

Peel cucumbers and score the outside with a fork. Cut the cucumbers in half lengthwise, scoop out the seeds, then slice them ¼-inch thick. Set some slices aside for garnish. Combine everything in a medium serving bowl. Add the egg chunks last, tossing them carefully to keep them intact. Garnish the top with reserved cucumber slices and parsley. Serve chilled.

Yield: 4 servings
Calories: 187/serving

Keith often visits his farm, which is an hour's drive from Dallas.

PLATEAUS

As a result of training, progress should be both steady and rapid, as it will be if the guidelines offered in this book are understood and followed. Viewed on a month-to-month basis, occasional sticking points or plateaus will probably be encountered. Usually, a plateau is a direct result of overtraining, which can be sidetracked by a brief layoff. In some cases another remedy must be found.

On encountering a stubborn sticking point, many bodybuilders eventually assume that they have reached their genetic potential. Almost always, they are wrong. The potential levels of attainment are so high that few individuals ever approach them.

When a plateau is experienced that will not respond to a brief layoff, or when a plateau is encountered immediately following a layoff, then one of two possible methods will probably end it. For example, if you are stuck on 7 repetitions in the curl with a resistance of 100 pounds, the weight should be increased to 105 pounds. This extra weight will probably reduce your curling ability so that you can do only three or four repetitions. But if you perform all of your exercises as *maximum possible sets*, you will make progress. And soon, experience indicates, you will be able to perform 8 or more repetitions with the 105-pound weight.

Another plateau-busting remedy: simply stop doing the unproductive exercise and find a similar one to replace it.

If none of these methods—layoffs, increased resistance, or substitution of a similar exercise—produce the desired result, overtraining should be suspected. But do not take a layoff—at least not yet. If 12 exercises are being performed, try reducing the number to 10 and/or reducing the weekly workouts.

If the results are still not forthcoming, the fault usually will be due to the maturity factor. In other words, you simply may be too young. For example, bodybuilders between the ages of 25 and 35 usually get better results than those between the ages of 15 and 25.

Total failure to produce continuing progress is almost never encountered. When it is, you are probably suffering from an undetected illness or failing to devote the proper intensity of effort to your workouts.

DAY 28

Sundays are usually a time for reading, studying, and relaxing.

DAY 28 RECORD

KEITH'S SCHEDULE

8:00am	Wake up!
8:15am	Eat Meal 1.
8:30am	Read newspaper.
10:00am	Eat Meal 2.
10:30am	Attend church.
12:30pm	Eat buffet brunch, Meals 3 & 4.
1:30pm	Return home.
2:00pm	Watch TV.
4:00pm	Take a nap.
5:30pm	Enjoy drive or walk.
7:00pm	Eat Meal 5.
7:30pm	Relax or prepare for next day.
10:00pm	Eat Meal 6.
10:30pm	Bedtime.

YOUR SCHEDULE

YOUR CALORIES

TURKEY HASH

- 1 tablespoon safflower oil
- 1 large white onion, chopped
- 1 clove fresh garlic, pressed
- ½ red bell pepper, finely diced
- 2 medium potatoes, peeled and cut into ½-inch cubes
- 1 pound cooked turkey pieces, chopped
  Dash of Worcestershire sauce
  Pinch of cayenne pepper
  Salt to taste

Heat oil in a large skillet and sauté onion, garlic, and bell pepper until semi-soft. Add potatoes and toss over a medium heat for 8–10 minutes until potatoes are done and slightly browned. Add turkey and seasonings and stir for several minutes more until heated through.

Yield: 4 servings
Calories: 310/serving

FRESH PEACH CRUMBLE

- 2 cups peeled, sliced peaches
- 2 teaspoons lemon juice
- ½ teaspoon almond extract
- 2 tablespoons sugar
- ⅓ cup whole wheat flour
- ½ cup finely packed brown sugar
- 2 teaspoons safflower oil
- ½ teaspoon ground cinnamon
- 2 tablespoons chopped blanched almonds

Preheat oven to 375°F. Mix peaches, lemon juice, almond extract, and sugar in a large bowl. Transfer to a 9 × 5-inch loaf pan lightly coated with non-stick spray. Bake 30 minutes.
   Blend flour, brown sugar, oil, cinnamon, and almonds. Sprinkle over fruit and continue baking until topping is lightly browned, about 15 to 20 minutes. Serve warm.

Yield: 4 servings
Calories: 191/serving

Sundays are also a good time for meal planning and food shopping.

Negative-only work requires 40 percent more weight than you normally use, as well as two spotters to do the positive part of the movement.

DAY 29

NEGATIVE-ONLY ROUTINES

Over the next two weeks, you'll be emphasizing the negative, or lowering, phase during most of your exercises. To better understand negative training, a discussion of various types of strength is necessary.

There are three types of strength:

- *Positive strength:* The muscle is shortening against resistance.
- *Holding strength:* The muscle is exerting force but very limited movement is occurring.
- *Negative strength:* The muscle is lengthening against resistance.

Assume that an average trainee can curl 100 pounds in a maximum effort. Therefore his *positive* strength in the curl is 100 pounds. If he can curl 100 pounds, then careful tests show that the average trainee can hold 120 in the midrange position. Thus his *holding* strength is 120 pounds. If he can curl 100 pounds and hold 120 pounds, research indicates that he can successfully lower 140 pounds in a smooth, steady fashion. So his *negative* strength is said to be 140 pounds.

The above example reveals that an average male bodybuilder can *hold* 20 percent more resistance than he can lift. He can *lower* 20 percent more than he can hold or 40 percent more than he can lift. Clearly, a bodybuilder's negative strength is much greater than his positive strength.

If skill is removed from a strength test, research reveals that increasing either positive or negative strength always results in a corresponding increase in the other. Super-slow training, which you have been applying for 28 days, emphasizes the positive phase of each exercise by requiring you to lift the resistance twice as slow as you lower it. The negative phase of a super-slow repetition is still important, but it is not as important as the positive.

Negative-only training, on the other hand, focuses primarily on the lowering part of each repetition. Since you are much stronger in the lowering phase than you are in the lifting portion, at least 40 percent more resistance should be used in negative exercise than you normally employ in super slow.

The objective of negative exercise is to lower very slowly a heavier-than-normal weight. To do so, you'll need one or two spotters to help you lift the weight to the top position. On the first several negative repetitions you should be able to stop the downward movement if you try to, but you should not try. Each lowering repetition should take from 8 to 10 seconds. After 6 or 7 repetitions you should be unable to stop the downward movement no matter how hard you try; however, you should still be able to guide it into a slow, steady, smooth descent. After two or three more repetitions you should find it impossible to stop the downward acceleration. Stop at this point.

The best repetition range for negative-only exercise is 6 to 10. When you can do more than 10 repetitions, up the weight at the next workout.

Here's your negative routine for the next two weeks. You'll be on a three-days-per-week (Monday-Wednesday-Friday) schedule.

1. *Leg curl, negative only:* With 40 percent more weight than you normally handle, have a spotter help you in getting the movement arm to the contracted position. The transfer, or handoff, of the resistance should be gradual. Lower the weight slowly in 10 seconds to the bottom. Repeat for 6 to 10 repetitions.

2. *Leg extension, negative only:* Have a spotter assist you in raising the movement arm. Hold briefly at the top and lower slowly in 10 seconds. Repeat for 6 to 10 repetitions. Move immediately to the squat racks.

3. *Squat with barbell:* You'll definitely require two spotters, one on either end of the bar, for this exercise. Descend slowly in 10 seconds. Signal your spotters at the bottom when you want their assistance and do the same at the top when you want them to transfer the load. Do not rest in the top position. Make the negative repetitions as continuous as possible.

4. *Overhead press with barbell, negative only:* This exercise is best done on a machine or in a power rack. In a seated position, have your spotters help you to the top. Your hands should be shoulder-width apart. Lower slowly in 10 seconds. Repeat for 6 to 10 repetitions.

5. *Upright row with barbell, negative only:* Your shoulders will really be stimulated after this exercise. Grasp the barbell with a narrow, palms-down grip and stand. Have your spotters assist you in lifting the barbell to shoulder level. Keep your elbows above your hands. Lower slowly in 10 seconds. Repeat for 6 to 10 repetitions.

6. *Pullover with one dumbbell:* Do the pullover in the normal, super-slow style. Afterward, quickly go to the lat machine.

7. *Pulldown behind neck on lat machine, negative only:* If available, use a bar with a parallel grip. One spotter stands behind you and helps you pull the bar behind your neck. Lower the resistance slowly in 10 seconds. Repeat for 6 to 10 repetitions.

8. *Bent-armed fly with dumbbells:* It's difficult to perform this exercise in a negative style. Stick with the normal super-slow protocol. Move from the fly quickly to the bench press.

9. *Bench press with barbell, negative only:* Don't be afraid to go heavy on the bench press. Lower the bar slowly in 10 seconds to your chest. Let your spotters assist you back to the top. Repeat for maximum repetitions.

10. *Biceps curl with barbell, negative only:* Have your spotters help you curl the barbell. Lower slowly in 10 seconds. Repeat for 6 to 10 repetitions.

11. *Triceps pressdown on lat machine:* Do this movement in the normal super-slow style. Quickly do dips afterward.

12. *Dip, negative only:* You can do the dip without spotters. Grind out as many negative-only repetitions as possible.

DAY 29 RECORD

KEITH'S SCHEDULE

6:00am	Wake up!
6:15am	Eat Meal 1.
6:30am	Read newspaper.
7:00am	Get ready for school.
7:30am	Leave for school.
9:00am	Eat Meal 2.
12:00	Eat Meal 3.
3:00pm	Leave school.
	Return home.
3:30pm	Eat Meal 4.
4:00pm	Relax or take nap.
5:00pm	Leave for gym.
5:30pm	Workout.
6:30pm	Return home.
7:00pm	Eat Meal 5.
7:30pm	Read, study, prepare for next day.
10:00pm	Eat Meal 6.
10:30pm	Bedtime.

YOUR SCHEDULE

KEITH'S CALORIES

MEAL 1: BREAKFAST

4 cups cornflakes	440
2 cups nonfat milk	180
3 ozs. Brown & Serve sausage	240
2 cups apple juice	240

MEAL 2: SNACK

2 cups lowfat yogurt with fruit	162
1 plain bagel	190
1 tablespoon Simply Fruit preserves	20

MEAL 3: LUNCH
Roast beef sandwich:

7½ ozs. roast beef	450
1 onion roll	200
3 ozs. cheese (swiss or cheddar)	300
Mustard	10
1 dill pickle	15
2 raw carrots	62
2 cups nonfat milk	180

MEAL 4: SNACK

½ 2,600-calorie shake	1,300
4 chocolate chip cookies	200

MEAL 5: DINNER

2½ cups Ravioli, with meat sauce	750
2½ tablespoons Parmesan cheese	105
2 cups sweet peas	280
1½ cups creamed corn	200
2 cups nonfat milk	180

MEAL 6: SNACK

½ 2,600-calorie shake	1,300
4 chocolate chip cookies	200
Total	7,504

YOUR CALORIES

WORKOUT NEGATIVE-ONLY:
Whole Body

EXERCISE	Keith's Wt/Reps	Your Wt/Reps
1 Leg curl, negative only	220/8	
2 Leg extension, negative only	265/8	
3 Squat with barbell, negative only	315/6	
4 Overhead press with barbell, negative only	200/8	
5 Upright row with barbell, negative only	150/8	
6 Pullover with one dumbbell	85/8	
7 Pulldown behind neck on lat machine, negative only	220/8	
8 Bent-armed fly with dumbbells	120/8	
9 Bench press with barbell, neg. only	350/8	
10 Biceps curl with barbell, neg. only	140/8	
11 Triceps press-down on lat machine	70/10	
12 Dip, negative only	Bdwt.+40/8	

DAY 30

SORENESS, CRAMPS, AND WATER

Negative exercise, if you are not accustomed to it, will make you very sore. The soreness results from several factors.

First, negative exercise involves more muscle fibers. Second, because of the greater number of muscle fibers, a deeper inroad into your starting level of strength is possible. Third, negative exercise provides more stretching to your muscles and connective tissues.

Negative-induced soreness is felt sooner than normal, positive-negative soreness. It not only occurs sooner, but it goes away faster.

Don't be afraid of the soreness. Simply work through it, and use it as an indication that you are stimulating your muscles to grow at an accelerated rate.

More rest on your part is an absolute necessity during periods of negative exercise. It is very easy to overtrain. Try to get to bed an hour earlier than normal, especially on your workout days.

Make certain you are consuming the required servings from the four food groups. Drink plenty of fluids and water. Water is instrumental in the muscular growth process. It also helps prevent muscular cramps. If your muscles are prone to cramps after heavy negative training, you probably need to consume more fluids. It is especially important to drink 8 ounces of cold water immediately after your workout and eat a banana or two.

The success of this program is dependent on your consistency, consistency in eating, exercising, and resting. Your body operates best if it is subjected to doing things at the same approximate time each day. Try to be on schedule, but at the same time remain flexible. There are certain unavoidable situations that will interrupt your planning. Anticipate and prepare for such situations and deal with them in a beneficial manner.

Drink plenty of water each day. Water helps with soreness and cramps, and is essential to the muscle-building process.

DAY 30 RECORD

KEITH'S SCHEDULE

6:00am	Wake up!
6:15am	Eat Meal 1.
6:30am	Read newspaper.
7:00am	Get ready for school.
7:30am	Leave for school.
9:00am	Eat Meal 2.
12:00	Eat Meal 3.
3:00pm	Leave school. Return home.
3:30pm	Eat Meal 4.
4:00pm	Take a nap.
5:30pm	Freshen up.
5:45pm	Watch TV.
6:30pm	Eat Meal 5.
7:00pm	Read, study, prepare for next day.
9:30pm	Eat Meal 6.
10:00pm	Bedtime.

YOUR SCHEDULE

YOUR CALORIES

POTATO ONION SALAD

6 medium-size red or white rose potatoes
1 large sweet red or white onion, sliced
1 cup lite mayonnaise
1 tablespoon each safflower oil and white vinegar
¼ cup fresh parsley, snipped
2 teaspoons celery seeds
½ teaspoon freshly ground black pepper
Salt to taste

Wash potatoes. Steam them whole with the skins on for 30–40 minutes (or pressure-cook them 5–10 minutes, testing them after 5 minutes). You may also cook them in a microwave oven for 20–25 minutes.

When cooked properly, potatoes should be tender on the outside but a little more firm toward the center. Since these 2 varieties of potatoes are rather thin-skinned, it's better not to boil them.

When done, let the potatoes cool, remove the skins, and cut them into large chunks. Combine all ingredients well in a large serving bowl. Cover and chill overnight for maximum flavor.

Yield: 8 servings
Calories: 172/serving

GREEN BEANS WITH BACON

1 pound fresh green beans, or 9-ounce package frozen green beans
¼ cup boiling water
1 tablespoon diet margarine
½ cup finely diced Canadian bacon
½ teaspoon salt
¼ teaspoon pepper
1 tomato, medium

Cook green beans in water until tender; drain. Melt margarine in a nonstick skillet and sauté bacon until brown. Add beans, salt, and pepper to skillet, and top with tomato wedges. Cover pan and heat through.

Yield: 4 servings
Calories: 88/serving

148

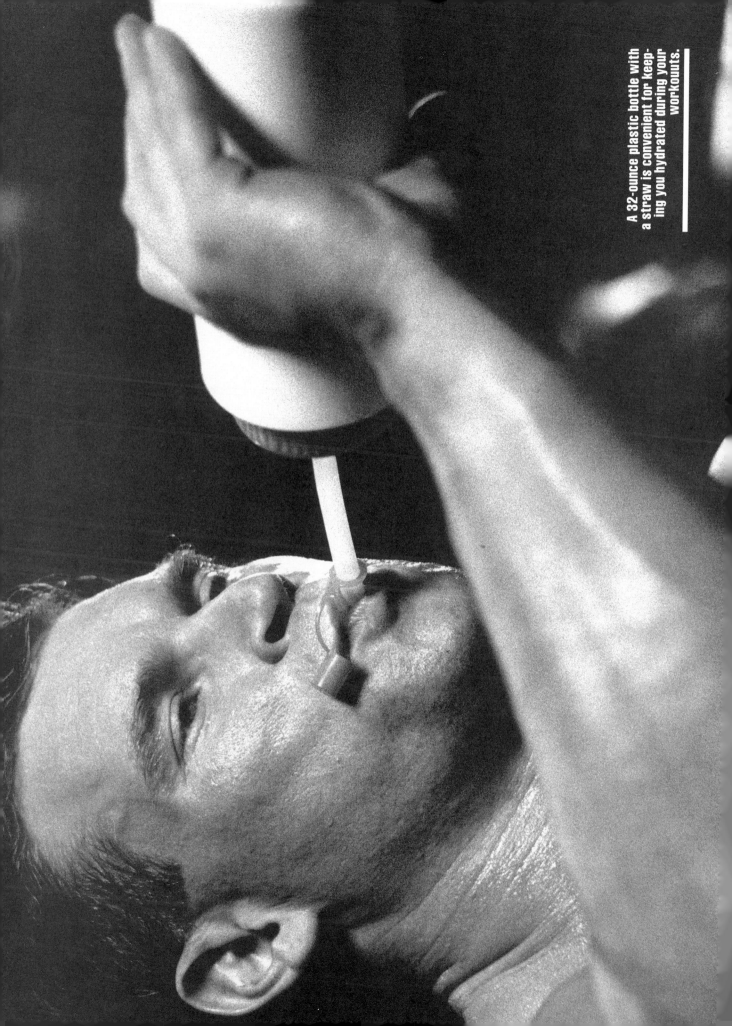

A 32-ounce plastic bottle with a straw is convenient for keeping you hydrated during your workouts.

INDIRECT EFFECT

Throw a rock into a pool of water and it will make a splash. A wave will run to the far end of the pool. The larger the rock, the greater the splash and the bigger the wave.

A similar effect results from exercise. This factor is called the *indirect effect*.

When one muscle grows in response to exercise, the entire muscular system grows to a lesser degree, even the muscles that are not being exercised at all. The larger the muscle that is growing, or the greater degree of growth, the greater this indirect effect will be.

Among bodybuilders, this effect is most noticeable as a result of performing *squats*. Performing barbell squats as a single exercise will induce large-scale muscular growth throughout the body. For example, if a six-foot man weighing 150 pounds is put on a regular schedule of heavy squats, he may gain 30 pounds of muscle mass within a year. All of this growth, however, will not take place in his legs and lower back. Considerable growth will also occur in the shoulders, chest, neck, and arms. This individual may have 13-inch upper arms at the beginning of his program, and at the end of his program his arms will probably be at least 15 inches in circumference. Other muscular masses exhibit similar growth to a greater or lesser degree. This happens despite the fact that no specific exercise was performed for the arms.

While it is possible to build various muscles disproportionately through the use of an unbalanced exercise routine, the body seems to have a definite limit on this imbalanced development. For example, it is almost impossible to build the size of the arms beyond a certain point unless the large muscles of the legs are also trained.

Young bodybuilders often ignore the training of their legs, concentrating instead on their arms and torso. Such a lopsided program will permit the arms to grow up to a point. Additional growth will not take place, however, until heavy exercises for the legs are added. Then the arms immediately start growing.

Working only the arms would have the largest indirect effect on nearby muscular masses such as the deltoids, pectorals, latissimus, and trapezius. This work would have the least effect on the gastronemius muscles of the lower legs. The indirect effect produced by building the arms would not be as great as that resulting from exercising the much larger muscles of the thighs or upper back.

The indirect effect depends on two conditions. One, the larger the muscle mass exercised, the larger the indirect effect will be. Two, the greater the distance between the muscle that is being exercised and the muscle that is not being exercised, the smaller the indirect effect will be.

Heavy, negative-only squats, more than any other exercise, bring into action the indirect effect.

DAY 31 RECORD

KEITH'S SCHEDULE

6:00am	Wake up!
6:15am	Eat Meal 1.
6:30am	Read newspaper.
7:00am	Get ready for school.
7:30am	Leave for school.
9:00am	Eat Meal 2.
12:00	Eat Meal 3.
3:00pm	Leave school. Return home.
3:30pm	Eat Meal 4.
4:00pm	Relax or take nap.
5:00pm	Leave for gym.
5:30pm	Workout.
6:30pm	Return home.
7:00pm	Eat Meal 5.
7:30pm	Read, study, prepare for next day.
10:00pm	Eat Meal 6.
10:30pm	Bedtime.

YOUR SCHEDULE

YOUR CALORIES

WORKOUT NEGATIVE-ONLY:
Whole Body

EXERCISE	Keith's Wt/Reps	Your Wt/Reps
1 Leg curl, negative only	$\frac{230}{9}$	
2 Leg extension, negative only	$\frac{280}{9}$	
3 Squat with barbell, negative only	$\frac{315}{10}$	
4 Overhead press with barbell, negative only	$\frac{210}{9}$	
5 Upright row with barbell, negative only	$\frac{160}{7}$	
6 Pullover with one dumbbell	$\frac{90}{10}$	
7 Pulldown behind neck on lat machine, negative only	$\frac{230}{8}$	
8 Bent-armed fly with dumbbells	$\frac{125}{8}$	
9 Bench press with barbell, neg. only	$\frac{365}{7}$	
10 Biceps curl with barbell, neg. only	$\frac{150}{7}$	
11 Triceps press-down on lat machine	$\frac{75}{7}$	
12 Dip, negative only	$\frac{Bdwt.+40}{9}$	

During negative-only dips, it is important to rest minimally between repetitions. Even a three-second pause means you are almost doing a series of single-attempt lifts. When you reach the bottom, quickly climb back to the top position and continue to lower slowly.

DAY 32

OVERALL BODY TRAINING

Understanding the indirect effect leads to several important conclusions:

- For maximum bodybuilding, your training program must be well rounded and must include exercises for each of your major muscle groups.
- The greatest concentration should be directed toward working the largest muscles of your body.
- The exercise sequence should be arranged so your muscles are worked in the order of their relative sizes, from largest to smallest.

In practice, this last point prescribes that your lower body be worked before your upper body. As a rule, your thighs are exercised before your calves, your back before your chest, and your upper arms before your forearms.

Since your waist muscles are used to stabilize your upper body in most exercises, they should be worked after your arms and forearms. The muscles on your neck, because of their critical location, should be exercised last.

The indirect effect is probably related to certain chemical reactions inside the working muscles. As a muscle works intensively, a chemical is produced that spills over and affects the entire body.

Since there is a limit to your overall recovery ability, and since many of your body's chemical functions affect the entire body, it should be evident that training every day is a mistake. That's why the program in this book gradually reduces your training frequency per week from six, to five, to four, and to three.

Three-times-per-week training, three overall body workouts per week, are much more result-producing—especially for advanced bodybuilders. Yet most bodybuilders of all ages continue to split their workouts and perform several times too many exercises and sets.

There are situations for split routines, such as those presented in this book, but these routines should be very brief and applied in the context of helping bodybuilders to understand that whole-body training three times per week is better in most instances.

Best results from negative-only training require that you exercise your legs before your torso, and your torso before your arms.

DAY 32 RECORD

KEITH'S SCHEDULE

6:00am	Wake up!
6:15am	Eat Meal 1.
6:30am	Read newspaper.
7:00am	Get ready for school.
9:00am	Eat Meal 2.
12:00	Eat Meal 3.
3:00pm	Leave school. Return home.
3:30pm	Eat Meal 4.
4:00pm	Take a nap.
5:30pm	Freshen up.
5:45pm	Watch TV.
6:30pm	Eat Meal 5.
7:00pm	Read, study, prepare for next day.
9:30pm	Eat Meal 6.
10:00pm	Bedtime.

YOUR SCHEDULE

YOUR CALORIES

CURRIED TUNA SALAD

   2 tablespoons lite mayonnaise
   ¼ teaspoon curry
   ½ 8-ounce can pineapple tidbits, drained
   1 7-ounce can tuna, drained and broken into chunks

In a small bowl, combine the mayonnaise, curry, and pineapple. Add the flaked tuna. If time permits, cover and chill the mixture to allow flavors to blend. Serve on a bed of lettuce of in a sandwich.

   Yield: 2 servings
   Calories: 220/serving

GOULASH

   1 pound extra-lean hamburger
   1 large onion, chopped
   ½ teaspoon garlic powder or 1 clove garlic, minced
   1 8-ounce can tomato sauce
   ⅛ teaspoon ground cloves
   ½ teaspoon basil
      Salt and pepper to taste

In a large skillet, brown the hamburger, onion, and garlic. Drain the grease. Add the tomato sauce and seasonings. Cover and simmer for 20 minutes to 2 hours (longer time yields better flavor).

   Yield: 4 servings
   Calories: 180/serving

MASHED POTATOES

   1 large (8-ounce) potato with peel, diced
   ½ cup water
   ⅓ cup nonfat milk powder
      Salt and pepper to taste

Cook the potato in the water in a covered pan about 15 to 20 minutes, or until tender when pierced with a fork. Do not drain the cooking water. With a potato masher or big spoon, mash together the potato and the cooking water. Add the milk powder and seasonings as desired.

   Yield: 1 serving
   Calories: 225

Shoulder shrugs, performed slowly and smoothly, not only work your upper back, but also your neck muscles.

STRENGTH VERSUS SIZE

For years, exercise physiology textbooks have stated that "the strength of a muscle is in direct proportion to its size." Unfortunately, many bodybuilders have failed to understand this concept.

An understanding of muscular size and muscular strength, in simple terms, is in order.

- To increase the strength of a muscle, you must increase its size.
- Increasing the size of your muscle will increase its strength.
- If all other factors are known and allowed for, a correct measurement of the size of your muscle will give an accurate indication of the strength of your muscle, and vice versa.

Once the above points are understood, the implications are obvious. Bodybuilders, who are primarily interested in muscular size, must train for maximum muscular strength to build maximum muscular size. Competitive weightlifters, who are interested in strength, must train for maximum muscular size to build maximum strength. In other words, bodybuilders and weightlifters should train in much the same way.

Much of the size-versus-strength confusion comes from the practice of comparing one trainee with another. Such comparisons cannot be done on a meaningful basis. Except in cases involving identical twins, it is scientifically impossible to make rational comparisons between two individuals. Even in cases involving identical twins, there are still enough differences to make many comparisons less than accurate.

This does not mean that you should not make comparisons. Meaningful evaluations can be made by comparing you to yourself over a certain period of time. Measurement of your body, before and after this 42-day course, can be valuable to you. Comparing your results to Keith's or David's, although interesting, can be misleading. Be careful.

In simple terms, neither the size of a muscle nor the strength of a muscle is an easy thing to measure. On a several-day basis, it's easier to measure your strength than your size. You're already doing a terrific job by keeping accurate records of your workouts. Each time you do exactly 6 repetitions of an exercise, circle it in red on your workout sheet. To be comparable it should be done in the same style at the same spot in the routine. If this is the case, then a gradual progression in your weight used indicates a gradual increase in your muscular strength. Likewise, there should be related increase in your muscular size.

Always move slowly and smoothly in doing the deadlift. Never drop the barbell suddenly or bounce it off the floor.

DAY 33 RECORD

KEITH'S SCHEDULE

6:00am	Wake up!
6:15am	Eat Meal 1.
6:30am	Read newspaper.
7:00am	Get ready for school.
7:30am	Leave for school.
9:00am	Eat Meal 2.
12:00	Eat Meal 3.
3:00pm	Leave school.
	Return home.
3:30pm	Eat Meal 4.
4:00pm	Relax or take nap.
5:00pm	Leave for gym.
5:30pm	Workout.
6:30pm	Return home.
7:00pm	Eat Meal 5.
7:30pm	Attend sporting event.
10:00pm	Return home.
10:30pm	Eat Meal 6.
11:00pm	Bedtime.

YOUR SCHEDULE

YOUR CALORIES

WORKOUT NEGATIVE-ONLY:
Whole Body

EXERCISE	Keith's Wt/Reps	Your Wt/Reps
1 Leg curl, negative only	250/8	
2 Leg extension, negative only	295/9	
3 Squat with barbell, negative only	335/10	
4 Overhead press with barbell, negative only	225/10	
5 Upright row with barbell, negative only	160/8	
6 Pullover with one dumbbell	100/10	
7 Pulldown behind neck on lat machine, negative only	235/8	
8 Bent-armed fly with dumbbells	130/6	
9 Bench press with barbell, neg. only	375/7	
10 Biceps curl with barbell, neg. only	150/9	
11 Triceps press-down on lat machine	75/8	
12 Dip, negative only	Bdwt.+40/10	

Keith Whitley has an excellent combination of muscular size and muscular strength.

DAY 34

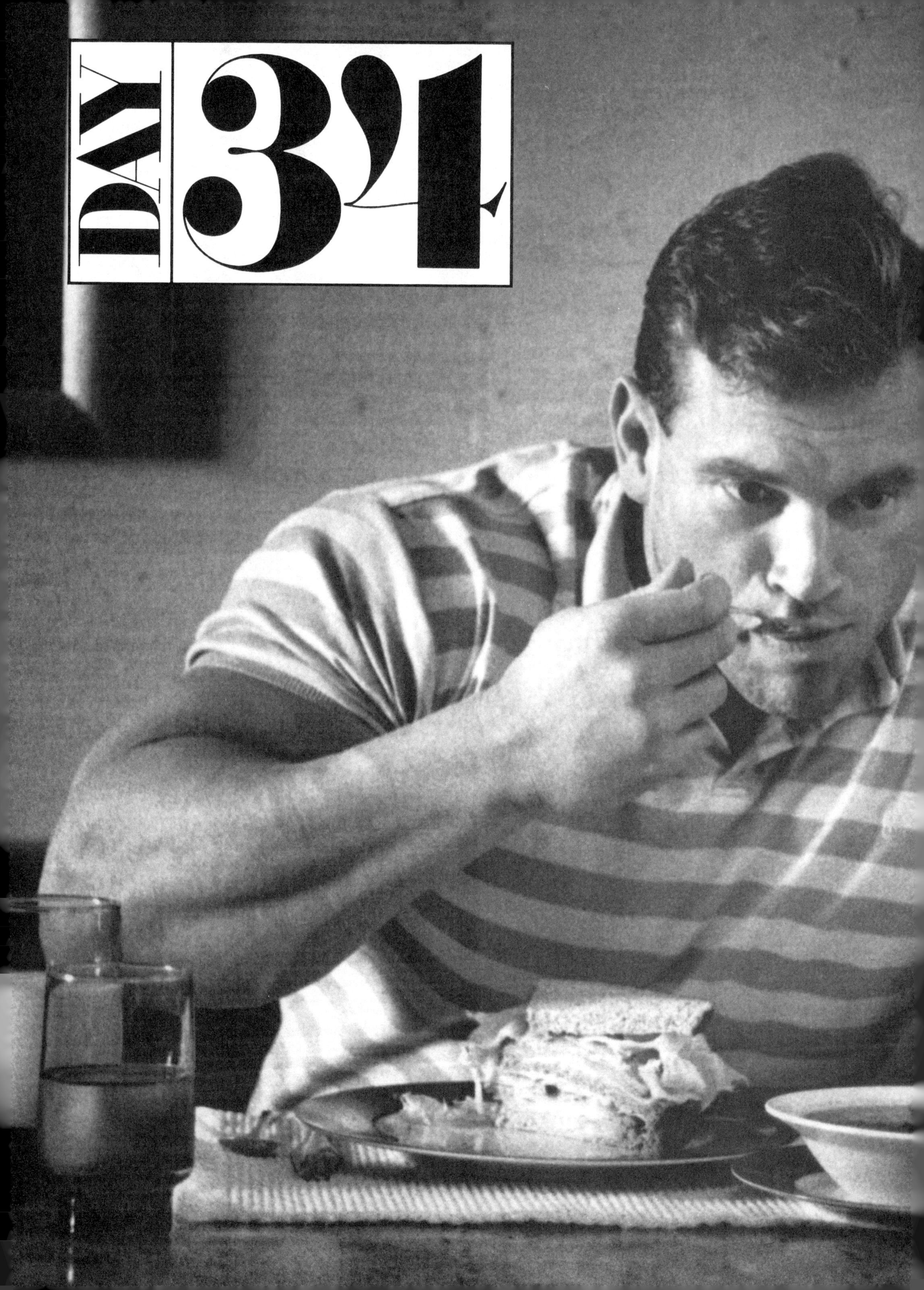

HARDER, BUT BRIEFER

A proper style of training is certainly not easy. It is much easier to do an extra set than it is to perform the last one or two hard repetitions correctly. This is especially true with negative exercise.

Those last one or two repetitions, however, are actually the only productive movements in the entire set. If they are skipped, the entire potential benefit of that set has been lost. The first few repetitions in a set are nothing more than preparation. They exhaust the muscles so that the last few repetitions can cause the overcompensation, or growth process, to occur.

Although most bodybuilders seldom exert themselves to that extent, they do work that hard at least sometime, even if only during one set a week. Most of their success is produced by those few hard sets. The rest of their training is wasted. It does nothing to stimulate size. That's why most bodybuilders experience such slow rates of growth.

Barbells are tools, and like any tool, they are subject to misuse. Barbells make it possible to perform exercises that are effective at building muscle. But owning a barbell does not ensure that a particular bodybuilder will understand the proper utilization of this tool. Nor does understanding guarantee correct usage.

It's possible to go through the motions of training as outlined in this book and attain little worthwhile results. Just as smearing a certain quantity of paint on a canvas does not create a meaningful painting, lifting and lowering a certain amount of weight will not necessarily produce gains in muscular size and strength. The significance of the painting and the lifting lies in how the paint is put on the canvas and how the weights are lifted.

Much of the *Bigger Muscles in 42 Days* concept can be reduced to two rules:

- Train *hard,* as hard as possible.
- Do *not* train too much.

Nutritious food complements your high-intensity workouts.

163

DAY 34 RECORD

KEITH'S SCHEDULE

7:00am	Wake up!
7:15am	Eat Meal 1.
7:30am	Read newspaper.
8:00am	Do home chores.
10:00am	Eat Meal 2.
10:30am	Wash cars.
12:00	Eat Meal 3.
12:30pm	Go grocery shopping.
3:00pm	Return home.
3:15pm	Eat Meal 4.
3:30pm	Take a nap.
5:30pm	Go out to eat Meal 5.
7:30pm	Go to movie.
10:30pm	Return home.
11:00pm	Eat Meal 6.
11:30pm	Bedtime.

YOUR SCHEDULE

YOUR CALORIES

SOUTHWEST CHICKEN WITH MONTEREY JACK AND PEPPERS

- 2 tablespooons fine dry bread crumbs
- 5 teaspoons chili powder
- 2 teaspoons paprika
- ½ teaspoon black pepper
- 4 chicken breast halves, skinned and boned
- 4 ounces thinly sliced Monterey Jack cheese, cut to fit pocket in chicken breast
- ½ red pepper, cut into ¼-inch-wide strips
- ¼ yellow or green pepper, cut into ¼-inch-wide strips
- 2 tablespoons minced fresh cilantro, oregano, or parsley
- 1 avocado, peeled, sliced into thin wedges
- 2 ripe tomatoes, sliced
- 2 teaspoons fresh lime juice

Preheat oven to 375°F. Mix bread crumbs, 4 teaspoons chili powder, paprika and ¼ teaspoon pepper. Place breasts smooth side up. With a long knife, cut a large horizontal pocket in each breast, leaving one edge intact so attached top can be flipped back.

Allow 1 ounce cheese per breast. Line pocket with ½ ounce cheese and arrange 2 rows of red pepper strips over cheese down length of breast, with a row of yellow or green pepper strips in between. Sprinkle with a pinch of chili powder, pepper, and cilantro, oregano, or parsley. Top with remaining ½ ounce cheese, fold breast over, and secure edges with 2 toothpicks. Repeat with remaining breasts.

Sprinkle half the bread crumb mixture on a dinner plate and completely coat 2 breasts. Repeat with remaining coating and chicken. Bake chicken, covered, in a large lightly oiled dish for 10 minutes. Uncover and bake 10 minutes more. Discard toothpicks; diagonally slice chicken into ½-inch-wide slices and fan on a warm plate. On the side, serve avocado and tomatoes sprinkled with lime juice and cilantro.

Yield: 4 servings
Calories: 410/serving

You'll get a tremendous
pump from the hard, brief
biceps and triceps cycle.

DAY 35

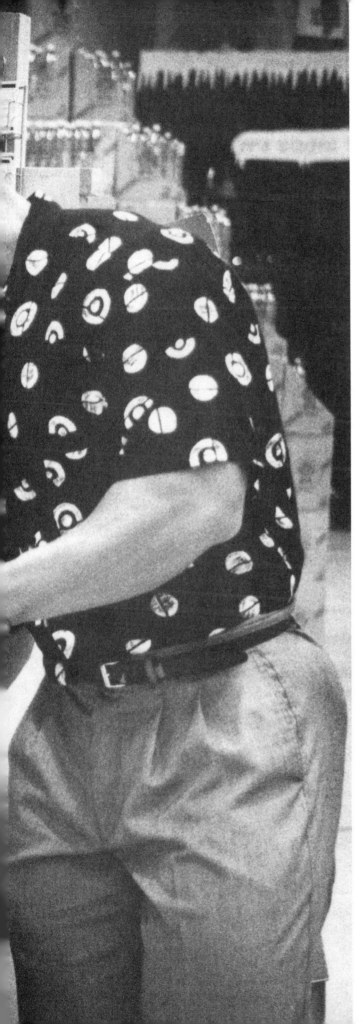

OVERTRAINING

Your muscles are capable of recovering from negative-only training in a very short time. But to obtain such rapid recovery, they must make demands upon the whole system, and your system cannot recover quickly. System recovery requires time. If a muscle is worked hard negatively, hard enough to stimulate growth, complex system recovery requires chemical action that cannot be completed in much less than 48 hours. For maximum growth, you may require as much as three days for system recovery.

If additional exercise is performed before system recovery is complete, muscular size and strength will be lost instead of gained.

The purpose of training is to improve your muscular size and strength. If that training is conducted properly, you should steadily improve until you reach your genetic potential.

The average bodybuilder is less than half as strong as he could be. He is nowhere near the size he could be. His training should steadily increase his muscular size and strength.

After an initial brief period of gains in size and strength, many bodybuilders make little progress. This should suggest that something is wrong with the program. Rather than doing less, however, they do more, progressively more.

One of the most common mistakes in bodybuilding is overtraining, gross overtraining, overtraining carried to ridiculous extremes.

You can easily overtrain if you do too much negative exercise. Include no more than 12 exercises in any one workout. Make sure you perform no more than three negative workouts per week. Two workouts per week, especially if you are already reasonably strong, may lead to even better gains.

Buying cereal grains in bulk is economical. Cereals are loaded with the nutrients needed to boost your system recovery.

DAY 35 RECORD

KEITH'S SCHEDULE

8:00am	Wake up!
8:15am	Eat Meal 1.
8:30am	Read newspaper.
10:00am	Eat Meal 2.
10:30am	Attend church.
12:30pm	Eat buffet brunch, Meals 3 & 4.
1:30pm	Return home.
2:00pm	Watch TV.
4:00pm	Take a nap.
5:30pm	Enjoy drive or walk.
7:00pm	Eat Meal 5.
7:30pm	Relax or prepare for next day.
10:00pm	Eat Meal 6.
10:30pm	Bedtime.

YOUR SCHEDULE

YOUR CALORIES

ROAST BEEF SALAD

1 pound leftover lean roast beef, thinly sliced
1 red onion, medium, thinly sliced
2 tablespoons safflower oil
¼ cup wine vinegar
¼ cup chopped parsley
1 tablespoon capers
1 teaspoon oregano
2 teaspoons prepared mustard
½ teaspoon garlic salt
¼ teaspoon black pepper
1 large head lettuce

Combine all ingredients except lettuce. Cover mixture and let it marinate in refrigerator for 3 hours or longer. At serving time, shred lettuce and toss with salad.

Yield: 6 servings
Calories: 286/serving

BANANA BREAD

3 large well-ripened bananas
1 egg or 2 egg whites
2 tablespoons safflower oil
⅓ cup milk
½ cup sugar
1 teaspoon salt
1 teaspoon baking soda
½ teaspoon baking powder
1½ cups flour

Preheat the oven to 350°. Mash the bananas with a fork. Add the egg, oil, milk, sugar, salt, baking soda, and baking powder. Beat well. Gently blend the flour into the banana mixture and stir for 20 seconds or until moistened. Pour into a lightly oiled or wax-papered 4″ × 8″ loaf pan. Bake for 45 minutes or until a toothpick inserted near the middle comes out clean. Let cool for 5 minutes before taking out of the pan.

Yield: 12 servings
Calories: 140/serving or slice

Too much negative-only work can lead to overtraining. Perform no more than 12 negative-only exercises in any workout.

Individual muscle fibers perform on an all-or-nothing basis. Only the number of fibers that are actually required to move a particular amount of resistance are involved in any movement.

In effect, a fiber is working as hard as possible or not at all. A movement against light resistance does not involve a small amount of work on the part of all the fibers in the muscles contributing to this movement. Instead, only a few fibers are involved—the minimum number of fibers that are required to move the imposed resistance—and the remainder of the fibers are not involved. But the fibers that are working are working as hard as possible—as hard as possible at that moment.

One individual fiber may be involved in each of several repetitions in a set of an exercise, but it will not contribute an equal amount of power to each repetition. The fiber will always be working as hard as possible—or not at all—but its strength will decline with each additional repetition.

In practice, a set might involve a number of fibers in much the following fashion. The first repetition involves 10 fibers, with each fiber contributing 10 units of power to the movement. The second repetition involves the same 10 fibers, which then contribute only 9 units of power each, and one previously uninvolved fiber—an eleventh fiber, a fresh fiber—that contributes 10 units of power, bringing the total power production up to the same level as that involved in the first repetition.

The third repetition might involve the same initially used 10 fibers, with each of them now contributing only 8.1 units of power, plus the eleventh fiber that was used previously only during the second repetition, and which now contributes 9 units of power, plus a twelfth fiber, a fresh fiber that is involved for the first time only during the third repetition and contributes 10 units of power.

Each of the first three repetitions, therefore, would result in exactly the same amount of power production. And all of the involved fibers would always be contributing to the limit of their momentary ability. The fibers, however, would not be contributing equally, and the actual number of involved fibers would change from repetition to repetition.

To produce significant growth stimulation, the set must be continued to a point where as many as possible of the available fibers have been involved, and where at least some of the fibers have been worked to momentary failure.

Negative exercise involves more muscle fibers, in comparison to normal positive-negative movements, and it works the involved fibers to a deeper level of fatigue.

In this final week of the 42-day program, you have three more negative workouts. Give each one your best effort.

Maximum-effort training merits high-quality food, and you should have your eating schedule in full force as well.

Your discipline and consistency are making you bigger by the day.

Keep going strong!

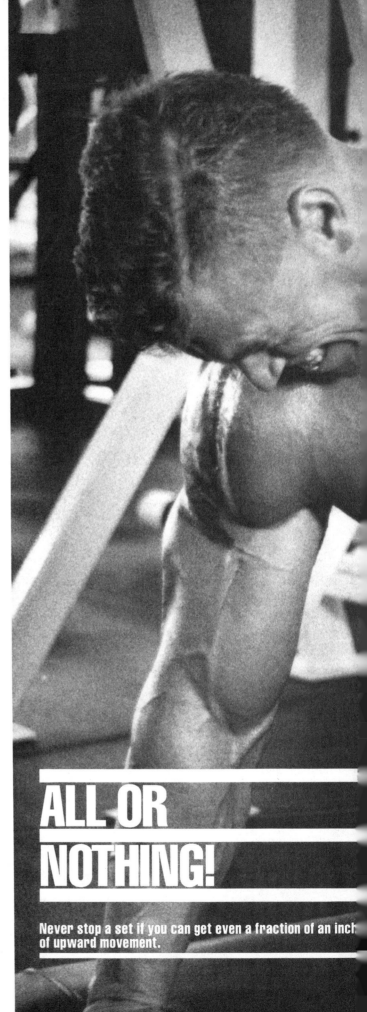

ALL OR NOTHING!

Never stop a set if you can get even a fraction of an inch of upward movement.

DAY 36

DAY 36 RECORD

KEITH'S SCHEDULE

6:00am	Wake up!
6:15am	Eat Meal 1.
6:30am	Read newspaper.
7:00am	Get ready for school.
7:30am	Leave for school.
9:00am	Eat Meal 2.
12:00	Eat Meal 3.
3:00pm	Leave school.
	Return home.
3:30pm	Eat Meal 4.
4:00pm	Relax or take nap.
5:00pm	Leave for gym.
5:30pm	Workout.
6:30pm	Return home.
7:00pm	Eat Meal 5.
7:30pm	Read, study, prepare for next day.
10:00pm	Eat Meal 6.
10:30pm	Bedtime.

YOUR SCHEDULE

KEITH'S CALORIES

MEAL 1: BREAKFAST

4 waffles (from frozen)	480
2 tablespoons syrup	105
2 teaspoons butter/margarine	70
1 cup orange juice	120
4 slices Canadian bacon	200
1½ cup nonfat milk	135

MEAL 2: SNACK

2 blueberry muffins	280
2 teaspoons butter	70
1 banana	100
¼ cup raisins	100
1 cup nonfat milk	90

MEAL 3: LUNCH

2 corn dogs	660
2 cups macaroni and cheese	460
2 cups applesauce	200
2 cups tomato juice	100

MEAL 4: SNACK

½ 2,800-calorie shake	1,400
20 pretzels (small sticks)	70

MEAL 5: DINNER

2 cups homemade beef and vegetable stew	440
Spinach salad:	
2 cups torn spinach	40
1 cup slice mushrooms	20
2 tablespoons Ranch dressing	40
2 cups brown rice, cooked	464
3 cornbread muffins	450
3 teaspoons butter/margarine	105
1 cup raw strawberries	45
1 cup nonfat milk	90

MEAL 6: SNACK

½ 2,800-calorie shake	1,400
4 chocolate chip cookies	200
Total	7,994

YOUR CALORIES

WORKOUT NEGATIVE-ONLY:
Whole Body

EXERCISE	Keith's Wt/Reps	Your Wt/Reps
1 Leg curl, negative only	$\frac{280}{8}$	
2 Leg extension, negative only	$\frac{325}{7}$	
3 Squat with barbell, negative only	$\frac{350}{10}$	
4 Overhead press with barbell, negative only	$\frac{250}{8}$	
5 Upright row with barbell, negative only	$\frac{175}{8}$	
6 Pullover with one dumbbell	$\frac{110}{10}$	
7 Pulldown behind neck on lat machine, negative only	$\frac{245}{8}$	
8 Bent-armed fly with dumbbells	$\frac{130}{8}$	
9 Bench press with barbell, neg. only	$\frac{375}{8}$	
10 Biceps curl with barbell, neg. only	$\frac{160}{6}$	
11 Triceps press-down on lat machine	$\frac{75}{9}$	
12 Dip, negative only	$\frac{Bdwt.+50}{8}$	

Strict repetitions lead to better muscle isolation.

METABOLIC WORK

You situate yourself into a leg extension machine with one goal in mind: to make the weight rise, then lower, and rise again, as many times as possible.

Isn't that what weight training and bodybuilding are all about? It's that simple, isn't it?

Not quite. There is some truth in your assumption, but a key point is missing.

Lifting the weight is *mechanical* work. More important is the *metabolic* work that is produced by your muscles involved in the exercise.

Your muscles produce force, and that's all they do. The force produced by your muscles often results in movement of a body part, and perhaps movement of a barbell, dumbbell, or weight machine.

But the end result can also be affected by kinetic energy or momentum, which are not a part of metabolic work. Metabolic work is your goal in any bodybuilding exercise, and it often results in mechanical work.

Recruiting momentum to create movement is not effective for overloading the muscle and thus stimulating growth. It's only good for explosive movement, which can be very dangerous. Jerking, lunging, and stabbing—slamming and banging—will damage your joints and connective tissues. Even if that damage is not apparent at the time, sooner or later it will take its toll.

Keep the muscle force flowing, whether or not the weight is moving. Keep it flowing steadily and smoothly. When it becomes nearly impossible to make the weight rise, just keep breathing and pressing into it. The weight may not be moving, but your muscles are working; they're producing force.

If you back off and stab, which is a release of tension in the involved muscles, using a little bounce (momentum) to move through the sticking point, your muscle-building benefit will be reduced.

An example might be a bicyclist at the base of a steep hill. Backing up to get at it will make it easier to pedal up the hill. But in proper exercise, you're not trying to make it easier, you're looking to make it harder and more effective.

Had you tried to pedal up the hill from a dead stop at the base, it would have required far more metabolic work, although by the time you got to the top of the hill the mechanical work would have been the same in either instance.

On any bodybuilding exercise, what your muscles are doing is far more important than the action of the barbell or weight.

Think in terms of metabolic work. When movement ceases, just keep pushing or pulling, breathe, concentrate, visualize it moving—and maybe you will get another repetition.

Holding motionless for 15 seconds the midrange position of a push-up is an example of metabolic work.

DAY 37 RECORD

KEITH'S SCHEDULE

6:00am	Wake up!
6:15am	Eat Meal 1.
6:30am	Read newspaper.
7:00am	Get ready for school.
9:00am	Eat Meal 2.
12:00	Eat Meal 3.
3:00pm	Leave school. Return home.
3:30pm	Eat Meal 4.
4:00pm	Take a nap.
5:30pm	Freshen up.
5:45pm	Watch TV.
6:30pm	Eat Meal 5.
7:00pm	Read, study, prepare for next day.
9:30pm	Eat Meal 6.
10:00pm	Bedtime.

YOUR SCHEDULE

YOUR CALORIES

BARBECUE BEAN CASSEROLE

- 1 16-ounce can red kidney beans
- 1 16-ounce can pinto beans
- 1 16-ounce can chickpeas
- ¾ cup barbecue sauce
- 2 tablespoons brown sugar
- 2 teaspoons mustard

Drain the beans. In a saucepan or casserole, combine the beans, barbecue sauce, sugar, and mustard. Simmer on the stove top over low heat for 15 to 60 minutes (longer time yields better flavor). Or bake in a 350° oven for 30 to 60 minutes; uncover the lat 15 minutes to thicken the sauce.

Yield: 8 servings
Calories: 200/serving

CORN BREAD

- 1 cup yellow cornmeal
- 2 teaspoons baking powder
- ½ teaspoon salt
- 1 egg or 2 egg whites
- ¾ cup low-fat milk
- ¼ cup safflower oil
- 1 16-ounce can cream-style corn

Preheat the oven to 350°. In a medium bowl, combine the cornmeal, baking powder, and salt. Beat together the egg, milk, oil, and cream-style corn. Add to the cornmeal mixture; stir just until blended. Do not overbeat. Pour into an oiled or wax-papered 8″ × 8″ baking pan. Bake about 40 minutes or until golden. Let stand for 10 minutes before cutting into squares.

Yield: 9 squares
Calories: 180/square

Fast repetitions involve excessive momentum. Excessive momentum transfers much of the resistance from the muscles to the joints and connective tissues.

DAY 38

RELAXING THE FACE

Effective workouts require an all-out effort. If the by-product of this effort is excessive facial contortions and continual grunts and groans—the effort is not as great as it could be.

Many small muscles of the face and neck contract when you grimace. This depletes a certain amount of energy. Conserve the energy so you can effectively work the muscle or muscles targeted by the exercise. Relax all the uninvolved muscles.

Making faces unnecessarily elevates your blood pressure. So does gritting your teeth and tightening your jaws. Since high-intensity exercise by itself elevates your blood pressure temporarily, there is no need to make it higher by making faces.

Grunting results from straining to force air out while your mouth and nose are closed. This is called the Val-salva maneuver, and is potentially dangerous.

The stress and strain of lifting a heavy weight can produce this type of breathing. The resulting compressed exhalation dramatically increases pressure in the chest area, cutting down the volume of blood returning to the heart so drastically that dizziness of a blackout can result. There's even a possibility that blood vessels could rupture.

Breathe rhythmically. Some coaches instruct power lifters to hold their breath, which creates a rigid rib cage and provides support for the upper spine. While this may work for maximum attempt, single-repetition lifts, it is not recommended for several repetitions. It is especially *not* recommended for super-slow training and negative-only exercise.

Learn to relax your face and breath appropriately during high-intensity exercise. Doing so will accentuate the muscle-building effect.

On all negative-only repetitions, try to keep your face relaxed. Doing so will allow you to concentrate more on the targeted muscles.

DAY 38 RECORD

KEITH'S SCHEDULE

6:00am	Wake up!
6:15am	Eat Meal 1.
6:30am	Read newspaper.
7:00am	Get ready for school.
7:30am	Leave for school.
9:00am	Eat Meal 2.
12:00	Eat Meal 3.
3:00pm	Leave school.
	Return home.
3:30pm	Eat Meal 4.
4:00pm	Relax or take nap.
5:00pm	Leave for gym.
5:30pm	Workout.
6:30pm	Return home.
7:00pm	Eat Meal 5.
7:30pm	Read, study, prepare for next day.
10:00pm	Eat Meal 6.
10:30pm	Bedtime.

YOUR SCHEDULE

YOUR CALORIES

WORKOUT NEGATIVE-ONLY:
Whole Body

EXERCISE	Keith's Wt/Reps	Your Wt/Reps
1 Leg curl, negative only	$\frac{295}{8}$	
2 Leg extension, negative only	$\frac{340}{8}$	
3 Squat with barbell, negative only	$\frac{360}{9}$	
4 Overhead press with barbell, negative only	$\frac{275}{8}$	
5 Upright row with barbell, negative only	$\frac{185}{8}$	
6 Pullover with one dumbbell	$\frac{120}{8}$	
7 Pulldown behind neck on lat machine, negative only	$\frac{255}{8}$	
8 Bent-armed fly with dumbbells	$\frac{140}{6}$	
9 Bench press with barbell, neg. only	$\frac{390}{6}$	
10 Biceps curl with barbell, neg. only	$\frac{160}{7}$	
11 Triceps press-down on lat machine	$\frac{80}{8}$	
12 Dip, negative only	$\frac{Bdwt.+60}{7}$	

Women often master the ability to relax their faces during high-intensity exercise better than men do.

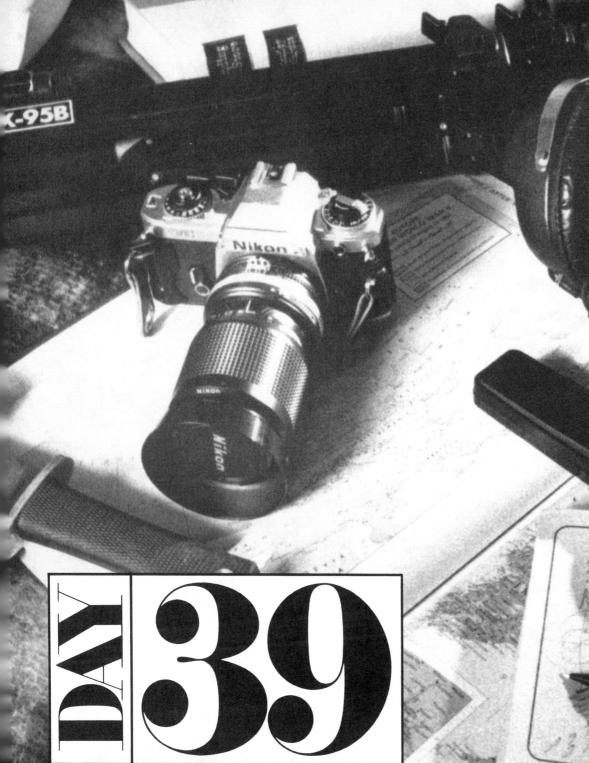

DAY **39**

NON-STRENUOUS HOBBIES

Leave your workout in the gym. Today's an off-day, so keep exercising out of your mind.

Too many highly motivated trainees spend the majority of their time thinking about bodybuilding. Thinking about bodybuilding is the thing to do when you're in the gym. In fact, the more you can concentrate on it during your workout, the better. But when you're outside the gym, direct your attention to other aspects of your life.

Become devoted to your schooling or to your job. Get interested in several non-strenuous hobbies, such as building model airplanes, playing a musical instrument, or collecting stamps. Visit the library, take a speed-reading course, correspond with a foreign pen-pal, or learn to speak another language.

You probably already have a keen interest in food and nutrition. You'd have to if you've been measuring serving sizes and counting calories for almost six weeks, right? Why not become involved in some of the speciality cooking courses offered in your community? Check the bulletin boards at your local newspaper, YMCA, and supermarket. Learning more about food and nutrition allows you to be more in control of your eating and well-being. Food preparation doesn't have to be all that complicated. Study it and profit.

In other words, get involved in other meaningful activities besides bodybuilding. Your stimulated muscles will thank you for it by growing faster.

Intense interest in a non-strenuous hobby can improve your bodybuilding.

DAY 39 RECORD

KEITH'S SCHEDULE

6:00am	Wake up!
6:15am	Eat Meal 1.
6:30am	Read newspaper.
7:00am	Get ready for school.
9:00am	Eat Meal 2.
12:00	Eat Meal 3.
3:00pm	Leave school. Return home.
3:30pm	Eat Meal 4.
4:00pm	Take a nap.
5:30pm	Freshen up.
5:45pm	Watch TV.
6:30pm	Eat Meal 5.
7:00pm	Read, study, prepare for next day.
9:30pm	Eat Meal 6.
10:00pm	Bedtime.

YOUR SCHEDULE

YOUR CALORIES

APPLESAUCE RAISIN BREAD

  1 16-ounce jar applesauce
  1 egg or 2 egg whites
 ¾ cup sugar
 ¼ cup safflower oil
  1 teaspoon cinnamon
  1 teaspoon salt
  1 teaspoon baking powder
  1 cup raisins
1½ cups flour

Preheat the oven to 350°. Combine the applesauce, egg, sugar, oil, cinnamon, salt, and baking powder. Mix well. Add the raisins. Gently mix in the flour. Stir 20 seconds or until just moistened. Pour into a lightly oiled or wax-papered 4″ × 8″ load pan. Bake for 45 minutes or until a toothpick inserted near the middle comes out clean. Let cool for 5 minutes before removing from the pan.

  Yield: 16 servings
  Calories: 145/serving or slice

OATMEAL RAISIN COOKIES

 ½ cup safflower oil
  1 cup brown sugar
  2 eggs or 4 egg whites
  2 tablespoons milk
  2 teaspoons vanilla
  1 teaspoon cinnamon
  1 teaspoon salt
  1 teaspoon baking soda
1½ cups uncooked oats
  1 cup raisins
1½ cups flour

Preheat the oven to 375°. Mix together the oil, sugar, eggs, milk, vanilla, cinnamon, and salt. Beat well. Add the soda, oats, and raisins; mix well, then gently stir in the flour. Drop by rounded teaspoons onto a lightly oiled baking sheet. Bake for 8 to 10 minutes or until firm when lightly tapped with a finger.

  Yield: 3 dozen
  Calories: 95/cookie

Strumming on a guitar won't develop your forearms, but it will develop a beneficial hobby.

CONCENTRATION

What is Greg Norman's demeanor when he's about to tee off, or Steffi Graf's when she's preparing to serve? Is Michael Jordan joking with his teammates when he's eyeing a free throw?

All of these athletes are in deep states of concentration. They're probably even visualizing the successful execution of their respective feats. Norman's golf scores, Graf's tennis ranking, and Jordan's point-per-game average would all suffer immensely if they did not put their minds into it.

Now, walk into almost any bodybuilding gym and what you're likely to witness is a romper room. Jokes, small talk, loud music, and goofing-off proliferate.

Your muscle-building benefits are adversely affected by a lack of concentration. You're hampering your goal of getting bigger.

To get the best workout you possibly can, you must concentrate. You must put your mind into it.

Bob Sikora, who often trains bodybuilders in negative-only workouts, allows no small talk during any of his exercise sessions. "I don't want to hear anything except what they're feeling from the movement," explained Sikora. "It's all business."

Ken Hutchins has coined a concept he calls internalization.

"Pretend that you are in a totally darkened room," writes Hutchins. "No sound—other than your own bodily functions—is heard. Your only communication sense with your body is feel. In the dark, you must imagine your body parts and what they are doing. This imagery is the basis for proficient motor control. It is also the foundation for superior mental control. It is required to perform internal muscular contraction."

Mental process is important. Going through the motions of an exercise means very little.

Proper exercise should be defined as *a logical strategy to bring about positive physiological change*. Your body's desire to maintain status quo makes producing change a very demanding experience. Healthy people aren't likely to think of such demands as being fun.

Proper exercise is brutally hard. An activity that is fun should be classified as recreation, with perhaps a small dose of exercise effect.

Betsy Hoffmann visualizes the set being performed successfully before she actually initiates the first repetition.

DAY '10

DAY 40 RECORD

KEITH'S SCHEDULE

6:00am	Wake up!
6:15am	Eat Meal 1.
6:30am	Read newspaper.
7:00am	Get ready for school.
7:30am	Leave for school.
9:00am	Eat Meal 2.
12:00	Eat Meal 3.
3:00pm	Leave school. Return home.
3:30pm	Eat Meal 4.
4:00pm	Relax or take nap.
5:00pm	Leave for gym.
5:30pm	Workout.
6:30pm	Return home.
7:00pm	Eat Meal 5.
7:30pm	Attend sporting event.
10:00pm	Return home.
10:30pm	Eat Meal 6.

YOUR SCHEDULE

YOUR CALORIES

WORKOUT NEGATIVE-ONLY:
Whole Body

EXERCISE	Keith's Wt/Reps	Your Wt/Reps
1 Leg curl, negative only	$\frac{310}{8}$	
2 Leg extension, negative only	$\frac{370}{8}$	
3 Squat with barbell, negative only	$\frac{375}{9}$	
4 Overhead press with barbell, negative only	$\frac{300}{6}$	
5 Upright row with barbell, negative only	$\frac{200}{6}$	
6 Pullover with one dumbbell	$\frac{130}{8}$	
7 Pulldown behind neck on lat machine, negative only	$\frac{265}{8}$	
8 Bent-armed fly with dumbbells	$\frac{140}{9}$	
9 Bench press with barbell, neg. only	$\frac{390}{9}$	
10 Biceps curl with barbell, neg. only	$\frac{160}{8}$	
11 Triceps press-down on lat machine	$\frac{85}{7}$	
12 Dip, negative only	$\frac{Bdwt.+60}{8}$	

Thinking about what you're going to do is an important aspect of the getting-bigger process.

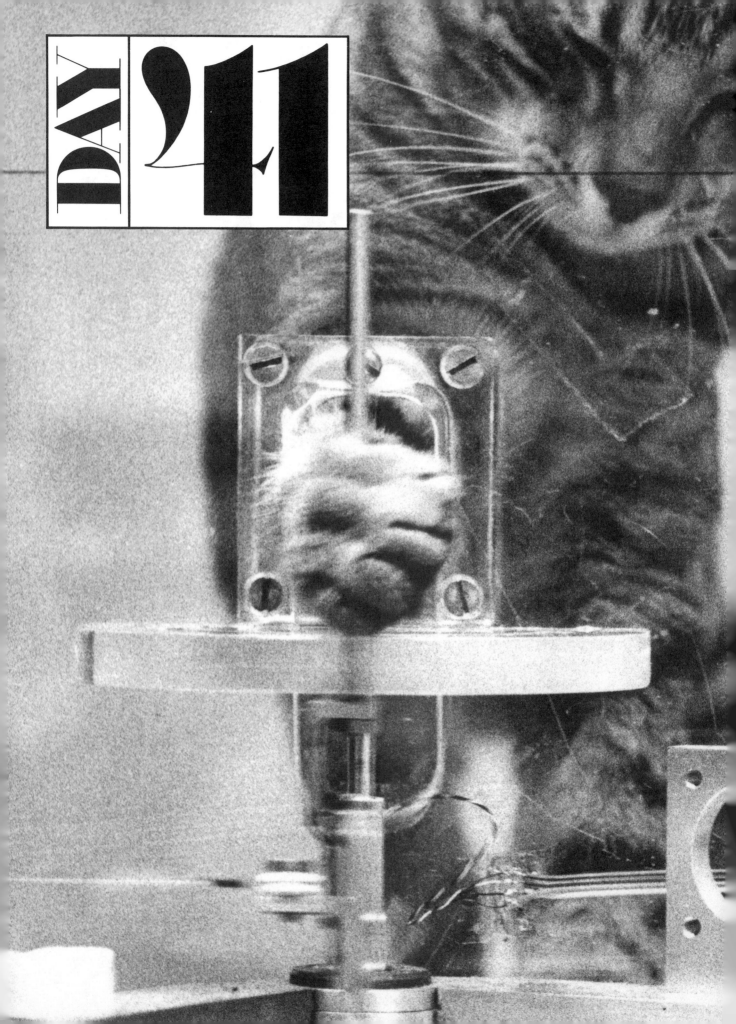

DAY '11

SUPER-SLOW CATS

Dr. Bill Gonyea has lifted weights for 30 years. He also is professor and chairman of the department of anatomy at the University of Texas Southwestern Medical Center at Dallas. For many years he has worked with medical students who are interested in exercise and muscle enlargement.

Recently, Dr. Gonyea reported the results of a six-year study with cats. The study was published in the *Journal of Applied Sport Science Research* (3:85–92, 1989). The findings will interest you.

Sixty-two cats were operantly conditioned, using a food reward, to lift weights with their right forelimb by performing a wrist flexion exercise. The cats reached through a tunnel in one side of a clear plastic enclosure and grasped a bar, which was attached to weights via a cable and pulley system. The cats then flexed their wrists against the bar, which lifted the weights.

The cats trained once a day, five days per week. All the cats began training lifting 100 grams. The weight was increased as the cats progressed. When a cat failed to make progress after a predetermined period, the muscles of the right and left forelimbs were removed and weighed.

The cats were not forced to perform by punishment. Thus, the intensity and speed of training was dependent upon each cat's personality and motivation for food. This in turn resulted in a broad range of performance values and muscle mass increases, which was accounted for with appropriate statistical analyses.

These statistical analyses revealed the following conclusions:

- The cats that eventually trained with the heaviest weights developed larger muscle masses in their exercised forelimbs compared to those that employed lighter weights.
- The cats that used slower lifting speeds developed larger muscles than those using faster lifting speeds.
- In the final analysis, the slower and heavier the lifting, the greater was the muscle mass increase.

Dr. Gonyea is convinced that bodybuilders can learn something from his study with cats. Bodybuilders should understand that lifting heavy weights slowly is the best way to increase the muscular size of a cat. *And* it is also the best way, he believes, to increase the muscular size of a human.

Of course you should already know this by now, right?

Zane, one of the experimental cats of Dr. Bill Gonyea, does a wrist curl with one-third of his body weight.

DAY 41 RECORD

KEITH'S SCHEDULE

7:00am	Wake up!
7:15am	Eat Meal 1.
7:30am	Read newspaper.
8:00am	Do home chores.
10:00am	Eat Meal 2.
10:30am	Wash cars.
12:00	Eat Meal 3.
12:30pm	Go grocery shopping.
3:00pm	Return home.
3:15pm	Eat Meal 4.
3:30pm	Take a nap.
5:30pm	Go out to eat Meal 5.
7:30pm	Go to movie.
10:30pm	Return home.
11:00pm	Eat Meal 6.
11:30pm	Bedtime.

YOUR SCHEDULE

YOUR CALORIES

POTATO PATTIES

- ¾ cup crushed bran flakes
- 1 tablespoon finely chopped parsley
- 1 tablespoon minced onion
- 2 cups mashed potatoes
- ¼ cup shredded Monterey Jack cheese
- ¼ teaspoon pepper

Mix bran flakes, parsley, and onion in a bowl. Set aside.

Combine potatoes, cheese, and pepper; shape into patties. Dip into crumb mixture to coat. Place patties on greased baking sheet and bake at 325°F for 20 minutes.

Yield: 4 servings
Calories: 140/serving

STIR-FRIED VEGETABLES

- 1 tablespoon brown sugar
- 1 tablespoon dry sherry
- 1 tablespoon soy sauce
- 2 cups broccoli florets and stalks
- 2 cups cauliflower florets and stems
- 1 teaspoon safflower oil
- 1 garlic clove, minced
- 3 green onions, sliced

Combine sugar, sherry, and soy sauce in a small bowl. Stir. Slice stems from vegetables diagonally and cut florets into 1-inch pieces.

Heat oil in wok or skillet. Add vegetables, garlic, and onions; stir-fry 3 minutes. Gradually add liquid and stir-fry another 3 minutes.

Yield: 4 servings
Calories: 77/serving

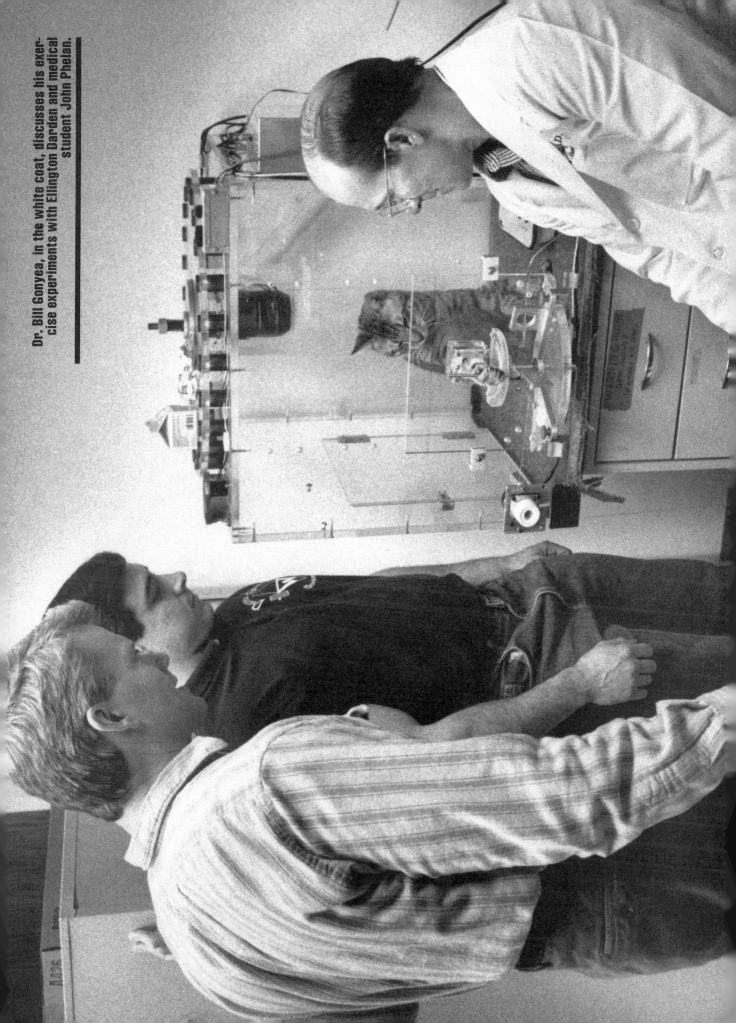

Dr. Bill Gonyea, in the white coat, discusses his exercise experiments with Ellington Darden and medical student John Phelan.

DAY '12

CONQUERING EMOTIONAL MOMENTUM

On this the last day of the 42-day program, it's a good time to review what has happened.

You began by accurately taking measurements of your body and estimating your metabolic rate. Then you planned a progressive eating plan where you gradually added calories to your diet each week. Combined with eating was a six-week exercising and resting program. Each day for 42 days you were specifically guided through an accelerated muscle-building course.

By now your muscles should definitely be bigger. How much larger are they? You'll find out tomorrow as you go through the post-measurements and evaluation section.

In the meantime you're to be commended for completing a very difficult training program. You've used the super-slow style almost exclusively for six weeks. As you know well, super-slow eliminates momentum, and momentum is the impetus gained by movement.

Momentum can also transcend to your emotions, says super-slow trainee Stephen Wedan, who also writes for several bodybuilding magazines. "It is comfortable to drift along, even when that something we're doing does not work very well. Drifting keeps people in unhealthy relationships because the world is a cold place to be alone in. It can also keep smart people in oppressive working surroundings because 'what if my brilliant ideas don't succeed out there?' And it undergirds the traditions in the gym, even if the traditions have not proved to be of much help!

"It takes guts to change direction," Wedan continues, "especially in bodybuilding. The proof of new ways of thinking may be there, but it seems often times so far away. And what will I look like in the gym if I'm the only one putting a different set of rules into use?"

Wedan is right on the money with his thinking. No doubt you've experienced ridicule by utilizing the super-slow protocol in your gym. It certainly isn't satisfying to have to lighten the weight, at first, in all your exercises. And those contra-lateral routines can really get some stares, can't they?

Keith, David, and I experienced the stares and comments too. But when something works as well as this program does, you can withstand such behavior. We did—and you did.

As Mike Mentzer, former Mr. American and Mr. Universe, often says:

"I know that it is difficult to accept ideas that are new, especially if they happen to challenge that which is near and dear to you. But remember—if you want to lead the orchestra, you have to turn your back on the crowd."

When a program produces significant results, you can withstand the stares and comments.

DAY 42 RECORD

KEITH'S SCHEDULE

8:00am	Wake up!
8:15am	Eat Meal 1.
8:30am	Read newspaper.
10:00am	Eat Meal 2.
10:30am	Attend church.
12:30pm	Eat buffet brunch, Meals 3 & 4.
1:30pm	Return home.
2:00pm	Watch TV.
4:00pm	Take a nap.
5:30pm	Enjoy drive or walk.
7:00pm	Eat Meal 5.
7:30pm	Relax or prepare for next day.
10:00pm	Eat Meal 6.
10:30pm	Bedtime.

YOUR SCHEDULE

YOUR CALORIES

SPANISH RICE

1 tablespoon diet margarine
1½ cups chopped onion
1 cup uncooked converted white rice
1 cup chopped green pepper
1 cup chopped celery
1 teaspoon chili powder
1 8-ounce can whole tomatoes, chopped
1 teaspoon salt
2 cups water
3 tablespoons bacon bits

Melt margarine in a heavy skillet, and sauté onion. Stir in rice, green pepper, celery, chili powder, tomatoes, and salt. Add water. Bring mixture to a boil; reduce heat and simmer, uncovered, for 20 minutes until liquid is absorbed and rice is cooked. Garnish with bacon bits.

Yield: 8 servings
Calories: 116/serving

BRAN MUFFINS

½ cup low-fat milk mixed with 1 teaspoon vinegar
1½ cups All-Bran cereal
1 cup hot water
⅓ cup honey
¼ cup safflower oil
½ teaspoon salt
1 egg or 2 egg whites, beaten
1 teaspoon baking soda
1½ cups flour

Preheat the oven to 400°. Line muffin tins with paper baking cups (or use nonstick muffin pans). Make buttermilk by mixing the milk and vinegar. Let stand for 5 to 10 minutes. Combine the bran cereal, hot water, honey, oil, salt, and egg. Let stand for 1 to 2 minutes. Add buttermilk, then the flour with baking soda stirred into it. Mix gently. Fill the muffin cups ⅔ full. Bake for 20 to 25 minutes.

Yield: 12 muffins
Calories: 160/muffin

Don't be afraid to turn your back on gym traditions.

BIGGER
BODIES

At the end of the 42-day program, Keith's left upper arm measured 20⅜ inches. That's a gain of 1¾ inches in six weeks.

Great! You've finished the program and you deserve a reward. Let me treat you to the most expensive buffet dinner in town. Please charge it to my American Express card. The number is . . .

Seriously, I wish I could buy you and all the participants in the BIGGER MUSCLES program a special dinner. You certainly have earned it. Your greatest reward, however, is the muscle you've built.

Turn back now to the measurement section and get your training partner to measure you in the same sites as before. Record your "after" measurements next to the "before" measurements on page 28. Determine the difference between each pair. Compare your results with Keith's and David's.

KEITH'S AND DAVID'S RESULTS

Below is a listing of Keith Whitley's and David Hammond's 42-day, before-and-after measurements:

KEITH'S MEASUREMENTS

Body Site	Before	After	Difference
Neck	16½	17⅞	1⅜
Right upper arm	18⅝	20⅛	1½
Left upper arm	18⅝	20⅜	1¾
Right forearm	14½	15¼	¾
Left forearm	14½	15¼	¾
Chest	50	54⅝	4⅝
Waist	34¼	37¼	3
Hips	43	44⅞	1⅞
Right thigh	28	29¾	1¾
Left thigh	27⅜	29⅛	1¾
Right calf	17⅜	18¾	1⅜
Left calf	17⅞	19¼	1⅜
Total inches gained			**21⅞**

DAVID'S MEASUREMENTS

Body Site	Before	After	Difference
Neck	15⅝	16¼	⅝
Right upper arm	16⅛	17½	1⅜
Left upper arm	16⅛	17⅝	1½
Right forearm	12⅞	13¾	⅞
Left forearm	12⅝	13½	⅞
Chest	39⅜	44¼	4⅞
Waist	32	34¾	2¾
Hips	40¼	42¾	2½
Right thigh	25½	27½	2
Left thigh	25⅛	27¼	2⅛
Right calf	16⅜	17⅛	¾
Left calf	16	16½	½
Total inches gained			**20¾**

Keith had an average weight gain of 5.7 pounds per week.

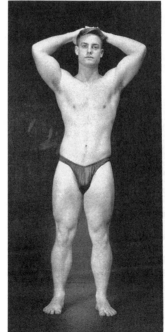
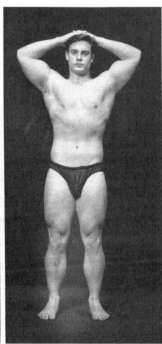

David's weight gain averaged 4.2 pounds per week for six weeks.

Summing the twelve before-and-after measurements showed that Keith gained 2⅞ inches throughout his body and David added 20¾ total inches. Most noteworthy among these measurements were those of the chest, thighs, upper arms, and calves. David put 4⅞ inches on his chest and Keith added 4⅝ inches on his. David increased the size of his thighs by 4⅛ inches and Keith improved his by 3½ inches. Keith gained an average of slightly over 1½ inches on each upper arm and David managed slightly less than 1½ inches per arm. Keith swelled each calf by 1⅜ inches.

MUSCLE AND FAT

Keith finished the program weighting 280.3 pounds, which was up 34.3 pounds from his starting body weight of 246. His average weight gain was 5.7 pounds a week.

David began the course weighting 186 and finished at 211.4 pounds. He gained 25.4 pounds in 42 days for an average increase of 4.2 pounds per week.

In charting the day-to-day body weights of each, it is interesting to note that Keith gained most of his weight during Days 1 through 25. Some of this could have been because he was overtrained and possibly dehydrated at the beginning of the program. David, on the other hand, seemed to gain steadily at the rate of from one-half to three quarters of a pound per day.

How much of Keith's 34.3 pounds and David's 25.4 pounds was actually muscle? Below are their before-and-after skinfold values.

Keith's percentage of body fat increased from 2 to 3.6. Multiply these percentages by his before-and-after body weights respectively and subtract the differences. Doing this shows Keith added 5.2 pounds of fat. Subtract 5.2 pounds of fat from 34.3 pounds of body weight, and his muscle mass gain was 29.1 pounds.

David's percentage of body fat, 11.3, remained unchanged. Multiplying this by his before-and-after body weights, and taking the difference between the two reveals he added 2.9 pounds of fat in six weeks. Thus, 25.4 minus 2.9 leaves 22.5 pounds of muscle that he gained.

In the final analysis, Keith gained 29.1 pounds of muscle and David added 22.5 pounds.

Keith's muscle mass increase was remarkable, especially when you consider that he was a national-caliber bodybuilder who has trained for over ten years.

David's was also impressive since he was a teenager who had been training only a little over a year.

If you have access to skinfold calipers, you'll definitely want to calculate your muscle and fat gains and compare them to Keith's and David's.

This day-to-day program has most definitely forced your muscles to grow. Now, your goal is to get EVEN BIGGER!

KEITH'S SKINFOLDS

	Before (in millimeters)	After (in millimeters)
Chest	1.5	2.0
Waist	3.0	7.0
Thigh	4.0	5.0
Total	8.5	14.0
Percentage of Body Fat	2.0	3.6

DAVID'S SKINFOLDS

	Before (in millimeters)	After (in millimeters)
Chest	7.5	4.0
Waist	18.0	20.0
Thigh	16.5	18.0
Total	42.0	42.0
Percentage of Body Fat	11.3	11.3

Successful bodybuilding is like successful living. You must plan, analyze, and adapt.

BIGGER THAN EVER

I've met some big bodybuilders during my life, and Keith Whitley is one of the biggest. But I don't remember a single one who didn't want even bigger muscles.

Getting even bigger muscles requires a continued understanding and application of the mechanics that you've used for the last 42 days. In short, you must have the correct blend of exercise, food, and rest.

I describe this correct blend in all of my body-building books, but especially so in:

■ *Massive Muscles in 10 weeks*
■ *BIG*
■ *Bigger Muscles in 42 Days*

If you've utilized one or more of those courses in the recommended manner, then your gains should have been significant and the experience should have been meaningful.

Such an experience can trigger a thought pattern that leads out of a blind alley. Having seen the results in your own body, you now have the chance to reexamine the involved factors.

DO IT. Do it now.

Reread this manual. Study the principles and guide-lines. Understand the harder-but briefer philosophy. Apply the super-slow protocol. Eat nutritiously and sensibly. Rest adequately.

Plan, analyze, and adapt.

You'll soon be bigger than ever!

TRAIN INTENSELY!

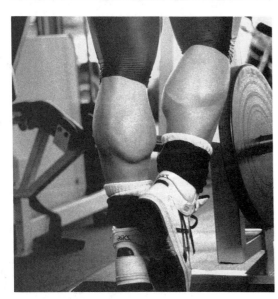

EAT NUTRITIOUSLY!

REST ADEQUATELY!

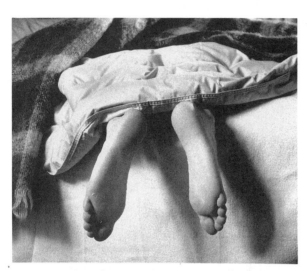

Now, your goal is to get
EVEN BIGGER!

OTHER BOOKS OF INTEREST

BIGGER MUSCLES IN 42 DAYS
   by Ellington Darden, Ph.D.   0-399-51706-5/$16.95

One of the leading authorities on fitness and bodybuilding provides a specific,
day-by-day instruction for achieving the ultimate physique.

THE GOLD'S GYM BOOK OF STRENGTH TRAINING
   by Ken Sprague   0-399-51863-0/$14.00

Long considered the classic in its field, now combines the latest technique and
technology with the time-tested methods employed by thousands of world-class
athletes.

THE GOLD'S GYM BOOK OF WEIGHT TRAINING
   by Ken Sprague   0-399-51846-0/$14.00

Contains the most up-to-date information on: developing a cross-training
program, choosing new equipment or a personal trainer and avoiding common
errors.

LIVING LONGER STRONGER
   by Ellington Darden, Ph.D.   0-399-51900-9/$12.00

Fitness expert Dr. Ellington Darden details how to start, continue and maintain
a life-extending fitness plan for the 40+ active man.

SPORTS STRENGTH
   by Ken Sprague   0-399-51802-9/$16.95

The founder of the world-famous Gold's Gym, Ken Sprague outlines stength-
training programs designed to increase speed, endurance and flexibility in this
fully illustrated guide.

TO ORDER CALL: 1-800-788-6262, ext. 1, Refer to Ad #593

Perigee Books
A member of Penguin Putnam Inc.
200 Madison Avenue
New York, NY 10016

*Prices subject to change